DRAMATIC ART

Theatrical Paintings from the Garrick Club

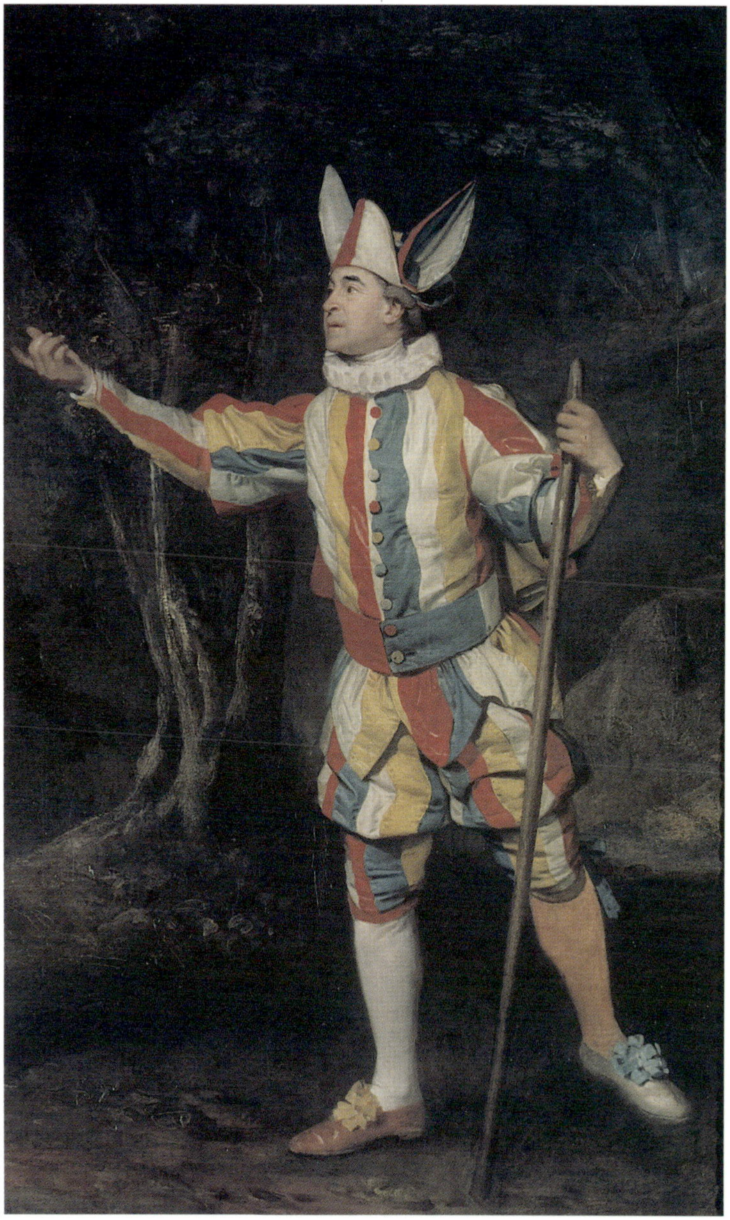

DRAMATIC ART

Theatrical Paintings from the Garrick Club

Desmond Shawe-Taylor

DULWICH PICTURE GALLERY

1997

This book was published to accompany an exhibition at Dulwich Picture Gallery, London, 16 January – 16 March 1997

Published by Dulwich Picture Gallery
College Road, London, SE21 7AD

Designed by Richard Beresford
Printed by The Lavenham Press

ISBN 1 898519 11 0

British Library Cataloguing-in-Publication Data:
A catalogue record is available from the British Library

Photographic credits:
Photographs are copyright of The Garrick Club/ET Archive (cover, frontispiece and Nos.1–41); All Souls' College, Oxford (Fig.3); Cambridge University Library (Figs.2, 6, 11 and 12); Helen and Richard Leacroft, from *Theatre and Playhouse*, published by Methuen, London, reproduced by permission of Reed Consumer Books (Fig.4); and the Trustees of the Victoria and Albert Museum (Figs.5, 7, 8 and 10). All rights reserved

Front cover: Johan Zoffany
Sophia Baddeley as Fanny Sterling, Robert Baddeley as Canton and Thomas King as Lord Ogleby in 'The Clandestine Marriage' by David Garrick and George Colman the Elder (detail)
The Garrick Club

Frontispiece: Johan Zoffany
Thomas King as Touchstone in 'As You Like It'
The Garrick Club

Preface

The theatre is part of the history of Dulwich Picture Gallery. The first-mover of the collection was the Elizabethan actor and entrepreneur, Edward Alleyn (1566–1626). A rare collection of portraits of theatrical personalities was assembled by the Restoration player-manager, William Cartwright (1607–86). Our founders, Sir Francis Bourgeois and Noel Desenfans, had close theatrical connections: it was recently suggested to me that their friend, John Philip Kemble (Nos.5 and 6), should be exhumed from his (apparently) inadequate Swiss grave and buried next to them in the Mausoleum's 'spare' sarcophagus. A group of portraits of the famous Linley family of musicians and performers, bequeathed by William Linley, complete our rich store of Thespian images.

If we are to be upstaged in this department it should only be by the Garrick Club. With nearly one thousand items, their collection is universally recognised as the largest and best in the world. Its core is the group of 235 paintings assembled by the comedian Charles Mathews (1776–1835). As well as containing some of the highlights of British genre painting, these images provide a comprehensive record of the actors and actresses; the plays and productions; and the sets and costumes of Regency theatre.

Our greatest debt of gratitude is therefore to the Members of the Garrick Club, for surrendering so many old friends for the duration of the exhibition, and especially to the Chairman of our Trustees, Lord Sainsbury of Preston Candover, KG, who first suggested this ideal collaboration between Gallery and Club. Of those associated with the Garrick we would like particularly to thank Martin Harvey, the Club Secretary; John Baskett, Chairman of the Works of Art Sub-Committee; Enid Foster, the Librarian; and Anthea Pelham-Burne, the Conservator, all of whose advice, encouragement and assistance we have depended upon at every stage of the preparation of the exhibition and its catalogue. I would like to single out the contribution of Betty Beesley, who has been tireless in her support of the project.

This exhibition would not have been possible without a generous gift from an anonymous charitable trust. The exhibition has also been supported with handsome donations from the Friends of Dulwich Picture Gallery and the Audrey Sacher Charitable Trust. We are most grateful to Richard Johnson of Stoll Moss Theatres for many helpful introductions and to the Museums and Galleries Commission (and especially Bettie Clark) for organising Government Indemnity.

This exhibition coincides with the publication of *Pictures in the Garrick Club*, a fully illustrated catalogue of the collection compiled and written by the late Geoffrey Ashton and edited by Kalman A. Burnim and Andrew Wilton. Our slim exhibition guide depends almost entirely upon the research contained in this catalogue: I am very grateful to its authors and to Hugh Tempest Radford for making proofs and photographs available. Our own catalogue has also benefitted greatly from advice from Linda Kelly, Sarah Stanton, Professor Peter Thompson and from research work undertaken by Lucy Till and Sophie Chessum. The design and co-ordination of the catalogue was carried out with efficiency and dispatch by Richard Beresford.

The exhibition was made possible by the dedication and hard work of members of staff at Dulwich Picture Gallery. Richard Beresford and Lucy Till have organised every aspect of the exhibition. Charles Leggatt has secured funding and Kate Knowles and Ben Rawlinson-Plant have arranged the extensive publicity and the events surrounding the exhibition, with the help of Francesco Nevola and Alison Mawle. The installation has been confidently handled by Alan Campbell, with the help of Tom Proctor and Stephen Atherton.

We have been most fortunate in the number of distinguished actors and actresses who have agreed to perform in the Gallery during the exhibition. Details of these readings are to be found in our *Programme of Events* leaflet. We are most grateful to the following for a generous donation of their talent and time: Prunella Scales, Crispin Bonham-Carter, Honor Blackman, Angela Thorne, Donald Sinden, Henry McGee, Rowland Davies and Richard Bebb.

Desmond Shawe-Taylor
Director, Dulwich Picture Gallery

Introduction

> But he who struts his hour upon the stage
> Can scarce extend his fame for half an age;
> Nor pen nor pencil can the actor save,
> The art and artist share one common grave.
> David Garrick, Prologue to
> *The Clandestine Marriage*, 1766

'The theatrical profession, unfortunately, is one made up of perishable properties'.[1] So wrote the actress Anne Mathews in 1838, despairing of ever describing her husband Charles's performances. The same thought lies behind David Garrick's affecting couplets printed above, with their deliberate echo of Macbeth's 'poor player that struts and frets his hour upon the stage and then is heard no more'. But Garrick and Mrs Mathews were both over-dramatising: the pen might not be much use, but the pencil (as a paint-brush was then called) could save an actor and his art. There are three actors who did more than anybody to commission and acquire theatrical painting. William Cartwright (1607–86) assembled a significant group of portraits of actors, including the only image taken from life of Richard Burbage (1573–1619, DPG395), the first Hamlet, Othello, Lear and Richard III. These paintings form part of Dulwich Picture Gallery's permanent collection. Cartwright's paintings are portraits; it was Garrick who invented stage painting as the depiction of a frozen moment of theatre. His artists (Hogarth, Hayman and Zoffany) brought their talents to the task, but the idea came from the actor. The only rival to Garrick in accumulating theatrical images is Charles Mathews, whose 235 works formed the basis of the Garrick Club collection, the best in the world for this unique genre of painting.

Of course theatrical painting is more than mummified performance. It operates on three levels: as an invaluable (though probably somewhat unreliable) record of an actor's style; as a comic commentary on the society which produced it; and as a work of art in its own right. This exhibition will take these three components in order.

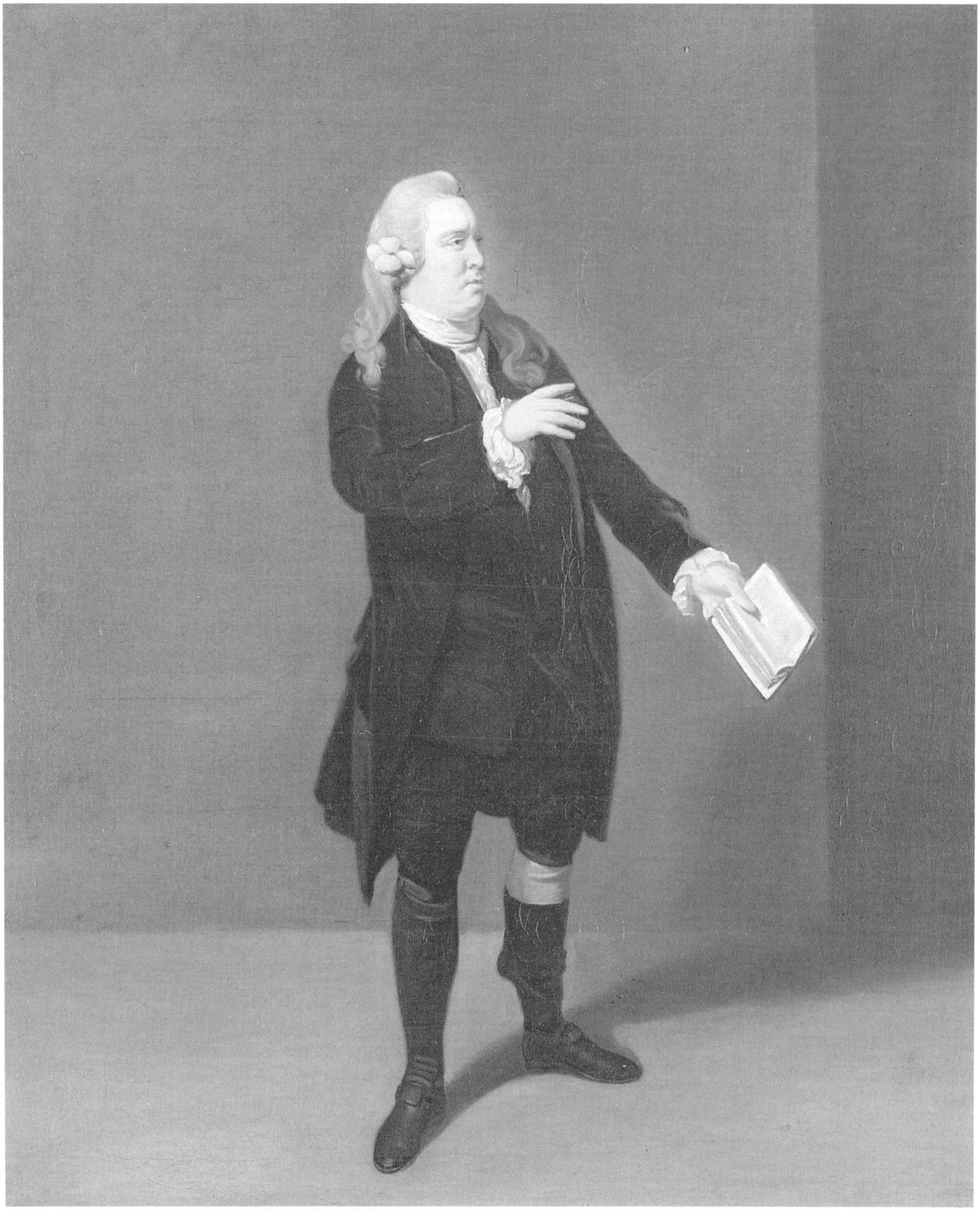

The Actor's Art

The first thing everybody comments upon when discussing actors in the eighteenth century is their deportment. In 1765 a talent-spotter reported to David Garrick on one James Dodd: 'his *person*', he writes, 'is good enough, but his motion ... [has] ... more the stalk and *menage* of a dancing-master than the ease of a gentleman'.[2] Dodd fails in something which cannot be *acted* and which it is probably too late for him to learn; he fails to be a gentleman. This is an age in which the children of nobility were sent at a very early age to dancing masters in order that they should learn not only to stand and gesture properly, but to look as if doing so costs them no effort or thought. Actors, especially tragedians, were required to demonstrate the same gentlemanly ease. Since they were not in the main born to it, this was some task.

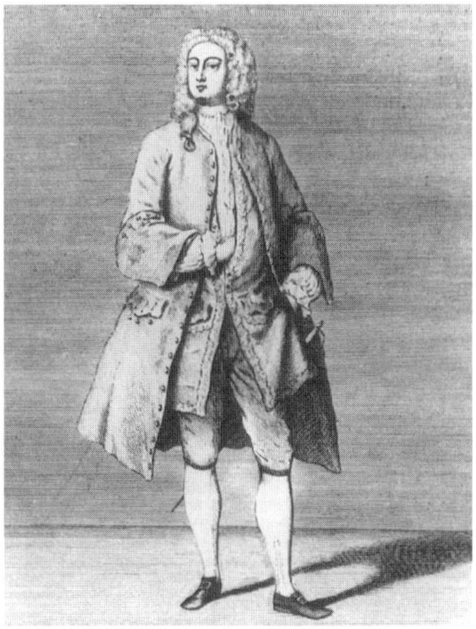

Fig.1 Plate from François Nivelon, *The Rudiments of Genteel Behaviour*, 1737

David Ross (1728–90) was in point of fact a gentleman (though a dissolute and disinherited one) and made a minor stage career out of his 'pleasing person and easy address', including regular performances as Hamlet at Covent Garden during the decade 1757–67.[3] The portrait opposite (No.1), showing Hamlet reading in Act II, scene 2, is more eighteenth-century gentleman than medieval Danish prince. The dress and posture can be checked against a popular deportment manual of the day, François Nivelon's *The Rudiments of Genteel Behaviour* of 1737 (Fig.1). Ross holds his shoulders back, gestures with elegant asymmetry and places his feet at the recommended (90°) angle to each other.

Of course he is a soul in torment, as can be deduced from the turning down of his left stocking. This was an accepted convention (also visible in Spranger Barry's performance, our No.35), which derives from Ophelia's description of Lord Hamlet:[4]

> with his doublet all unbraced;
> No hat upon his head; his stockings foul'd,
> Ungarter'd, and down-gyved to his ancle
> (Act II, scene 1).

Opposite:
No.1 Johan Zoffany
David Ross as Hamlet
1757–67
Oil on canvas, 77 x 64 cm
The Garrick Club

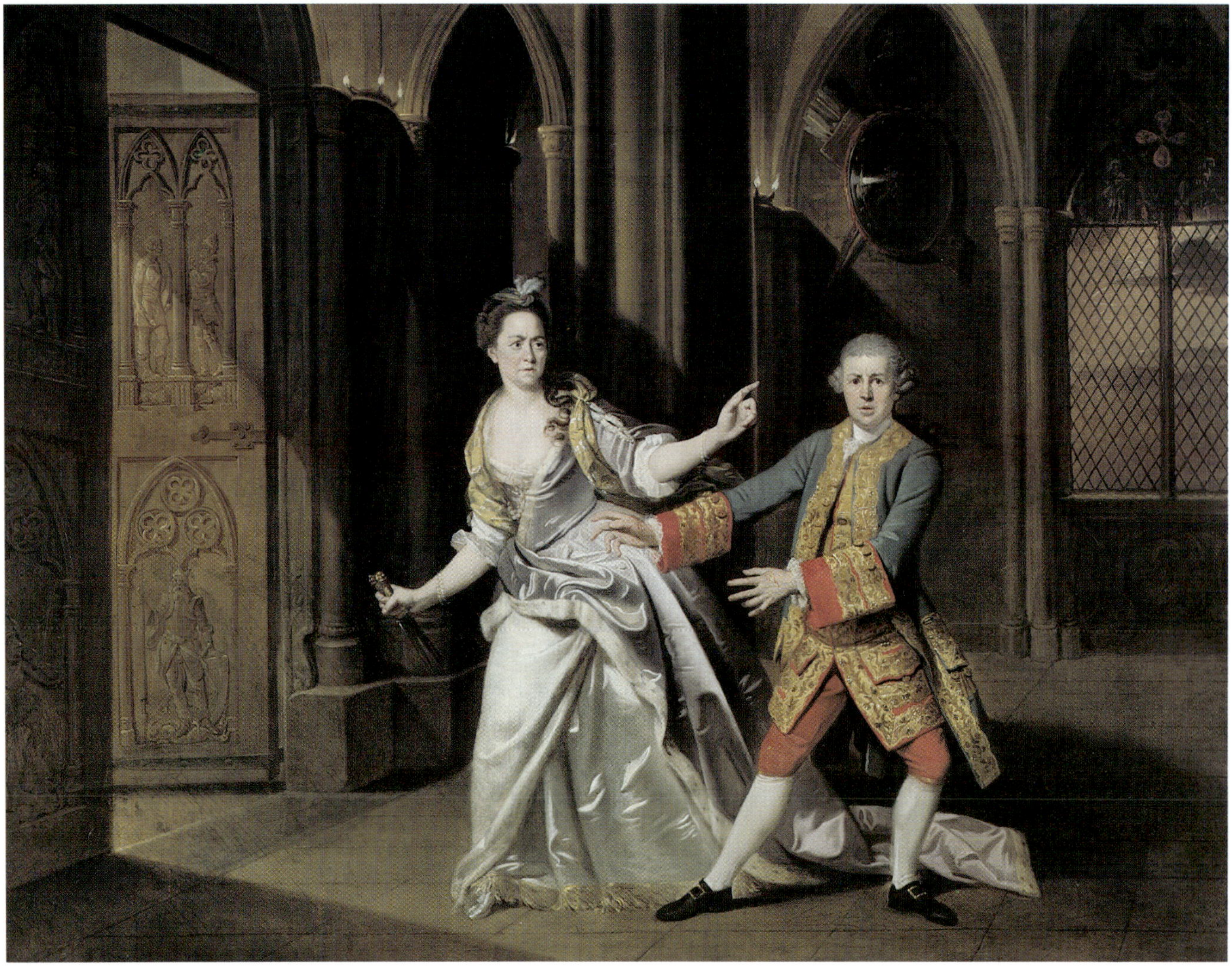

No.2 Johan Zoffany
David Garrick as Macbeth and Hannah Pritchard as Lady Macbeth
Oil on canvas, 102 x 127.5 cm
The Garrick Club

As down-gyving goes this looks rather token, but to follow the rest of Ophelia's account would have seemed hopelessly indecorous at the time. To audiences of the period Hamlet was in the first place a prince and only secondly a tortured soul. Later in the century Charles Kemble was particularly commended for those 'fine instincts' in his interpretation of the same part which 'taught him the unseemliness of launching bitter sarcasms at Claudius before his courtiers'.[5] We no longer think of such courtly 'seemliness' as an important part of Hamlet's character.

Though it may have been painted as late as 1760, Zoffany's image provides an insight into the acting style of the first half of the eighteenth century – there is certainly nothing to show that Ross had any awareness of his great contemporary and first employer, David Garrick. He looks like a left-over from the days when acting was more to do with impressive declamation than psychological impersonation. A performance in the 1720s or 1730s would probably have looked to us much more like an opera than a play. A treatise on acting written in 1755 recalled the forced gestures of the previous generation and their recitation which was 'a kind of singing'.[6] James Quin, the star of these early years, apparently spoke 'with very little variation of cadence, and in a deep full tone, accompanied by a sawing kind of action'.[7] These writers had learned to expect more, for they were living in the age of Garrick.

Garrick and the Natural Revolution

> Inimitable Shakespeare! but more matchless
> Garrick! always as deep in Nature as the Poet.
>
> William Pitt[8]

It was in 1741 that the British stage underwent its revolution, for in this same year Charles Macklin played Shylock at Drury Lane (see Fig.10) and David Garrick played Richard III at Goodman's Fields. David Garrick's person and deportment were up to the dignity of any tragic part – contemporary reviews commend the 'peculiar happiness in his address and action' – but he used them in a novel way.[9] As he himself put it, when he encountered the obsolete style still in vogue amongst provincial strollers, 'we in Town are Endeavouring to bring the Sock & Buskin down to Nature, but they still keep their Strutting, Bouncing, and Mouthing, that with Whiskers on they put me in mind of ye late Czar of Russia who was both an Ideot & a Madman'.[10]

What does 'bringing down to Nature' involve? Zoffany's depiction of Garrick in *Macbeth* may give some idea (No.2). He is playing opposite Hannah Pritchard's Lady Macbeth, a famous pairing which lasted from 1748 to 1768. Macbeth has just murdered Duncan; his wife urges him to return the daggers to the scene of the crime so as clumsily to frame the grooms.

Macbeth:	I'll go no more:
	I am afraid to think what I have done
	Look on't again I dare not.
Lady Macbeth:	Infirm of purpose!
	Give me the daggers (Act II, scene 2).

They are both still in the dress of the eighteenth century. In the first performance Garrick played the scene with unbuttoned waistcoat and other 'discomposures in his dress', but his friends advised him against repeating the rash experiment.[11] The revolution in acting style was more durable. Zoffany shows a posture convulsed with horror: the body recoiling from the death-chamber, arms seeming to fend it off, and a jerky awkwardness to the whole figure. A contemporary description conveys the effect of this scene: 'You heard what they spoke, but you learned more from the agitation of mind displayed in their action and deportment ... The wonderful expression of heartfelt horror, which Garrick felt when he shewed his bloody hands, can only be conceived and described by those who saw him'.[12] What Garrick brings to the part is an immediacy of passion: this moment's start of horror, which may soon give way to some other contrasting reaction. All accounts of his acting draw attention to this thoroughbred nervousness and alacrity of response. He was famous for his transitions from one aspect of a character to another.[13] As a demonstration piece he would in the course of five to six seconds alter his expression 'successively from wild delight to temperate pleasure, from this to tranquillity, from tranquillity to surprise, from surprise to blank astonishment, from that to sorrow'.[14] When he seemed to have aged prematurely, Dr Johnson had a ready explanation: 'his face has had double the business of any other man's'.[15] These descriptions convey something exhausting to watch, which is certainly how it struck the old guard. Theophilus Cibber, son of prime ranter Colley Cibber, saw in Garrick only 'his over-fondness for extravagant Attitudes, frequent affected Starts, convulsive Twitchings, Jerkings of the Body, sprawling of the Fingers, flapping the Breast and Pockets ... the Caricatures of Gesture'.[16]

Garrick's style did not just rely on instinct: he was well aware of the systematic studies of expression which were fashionable at the time. As a party piece, he used to wear the various expressions described in Charles Le Brun's *Conférence sur l'Expression* of 1698, a treatise constantly referred to by artists and actors in the eighteenth century (see Figs.2 and 11).[17] His 'heartfelt horror' in Zoffany's depiction – the face staring directly out of the picture, with knit brows, open mouth and wide eyes – comes straight from Le Brun's plate illustrating exactly that emotion (Fig.2). The chief similarity lies in the conventions of the illustration itself: the straight view, with incised expressive lines within the schematic rugger-ball, gives to Le Brun's treatise, Zoffany's painting and, by extension, Garrick's acting an air of diagrammatic precision, of scientific inquiry. This was how the treatise was viewed – as a kind of descriptive inventory of the soul.

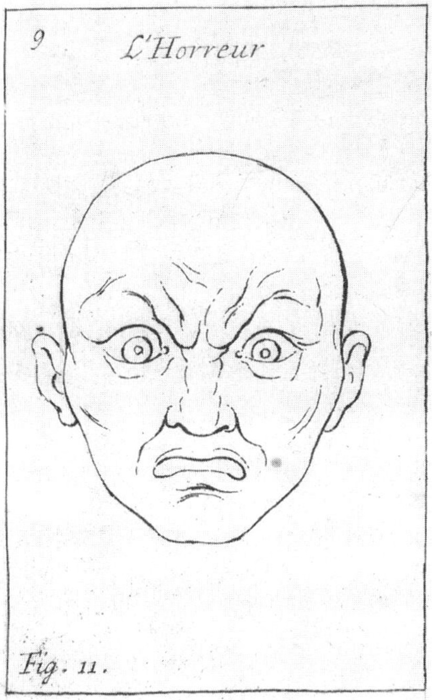

Fig.2 Horror
From Charles Le Brun, *Méthode pour apprendre à dessiner les Passions*, 1702
Cambridge University Library

Le Brun was important for the period because he represented a way of generalising the emotions. Charles Macklin felt that an actor should have a 'philosophical knowledge of the passions', knowing their '*genus, species* and characteristics' as a botanist might those of plants.[18] There is no limit to this over-rational pedantry of the passions: Aaron Hill's 1746 treatise on acting asserts that there 'are only ten dramatic passions', which he lists and describes so that actors may practise them in their mirrors.[19] Those lacking Garrick's natural talent might look up terror in Roger Pickering's *Reflections upon Theatrical Expression in Tragedy* of 1755, where they would learn that 'in astonishment and surprise, arising from terror, the left leg is drawn back to some distance from the other' and so on for the rest of the body.[20] The important thing for the eighteenth century was that generalising meant dignifying. A frightened man is contemptible; an artist revealing the secret principles of Terror is instructive and uplifting. In Zoffany's painting Garrick's features are generalised and dignified: they are expanded, regularised and given a sweeping pattern; they seem to be worn by the face like a noble mask. Even in the extreme of terror there is no contortion or grimace: Macbeth may be bad, but he's still a gentleman.

After an eighteenth-century audience had purged their souls with Pity and Terror by witnessing a tragedy, they settled down for a farce. This convention allowed Garrick to show off his renowned versatility (which incidentally was not shared by the other great tragedians in this section). One of the most popular 'afterpieces' of the period was Garrick's own *Lethe* (No.3).[21] Aesop waits at the frontier of the underworld and questions the characters in turn, before they drink the waters of the river of forgetfulness. Garrick played various parts in the play including the 'perservering debauchee', Lord Chalkstone, who was added in 1757.[22] Chalkstone is stubbornly cheerful: he dismisses the pain of his gouty legs and refuses to drink of Lethe, because there is nothing he wishes to forget. Aesop sums up: 'His Lordship here, supported only by vanity, vivacity, and his friend Mr Bowman, can fancy himself the wisest, and is the happiest of mortals'. Garrick brings to the part a kind of heroism of good-humour. A stick supports him, his splayed legs are rigid and bound in what look like thermal stockings, yet he faces eternity with a cheerful defiance. His quizzically raised eyebrows and smile give an air of wild bonhomie. A slight over-stretching of Garrick's maleable face and the rhetoric of tragedy becomes the mock-heroic of comedy.

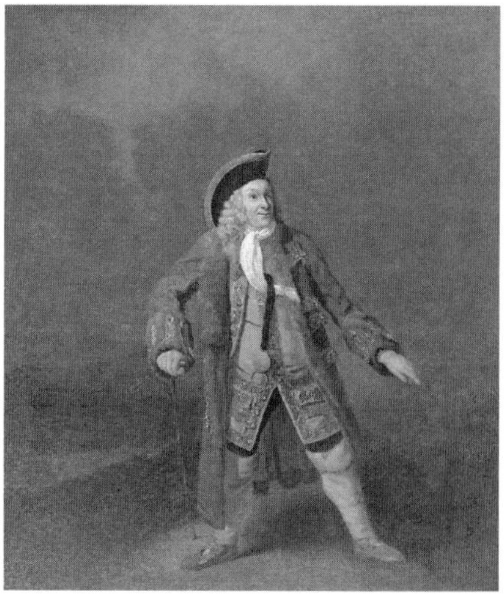

No.3 Johan Zoffany
David Garrick as Lord Chalkstone in 'Lethe or Aesop in the Shades' by David Garrick, c.1770
Oil on canvas, 76 x 63.5 cm
The Garrick Club

Sets

The Elizabethan theatre had no proscenium arch or moveable scenery; the acting area was a bare platform projecting into the audience. The seventeenth- and the eighteenth-century theatres in Britain never quite forgot these roots – Zoffany's portrait of David Ross (No.1) is especially suggestive of bare Elizabethan boards. A section drawing and reconstruction of Wren's Drury Lane Theatre, operative from 1674–1774, (Figs.3 and 4) shows that more than half of the acting area is to be found in front of the proscenium arch and moving scenery, in what was called the 'apron stage'. This area was flanked by doors for the actors and boxes for the audience.

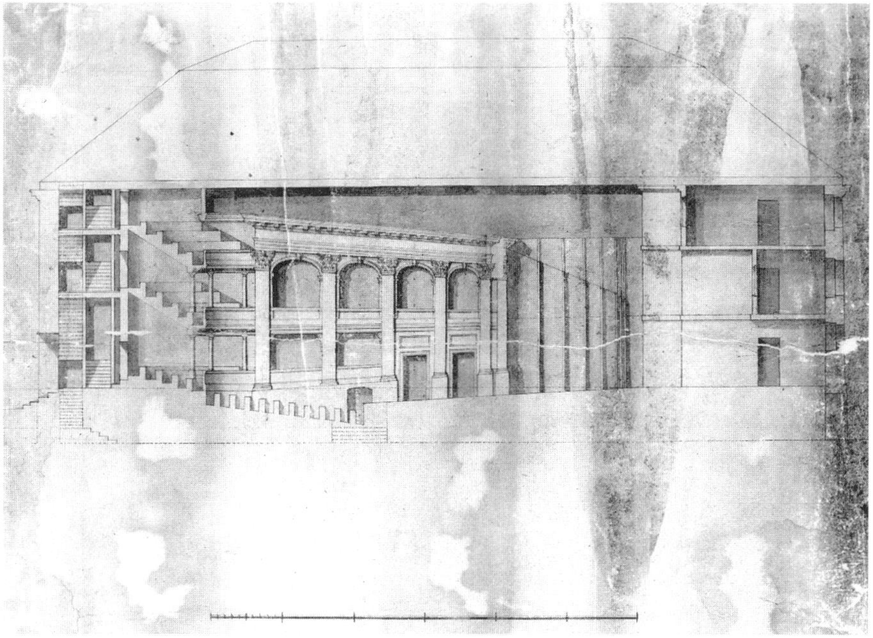

Fig.3 Sir Christopher Wren, *Section Drawing for Drury Lane*, 1674

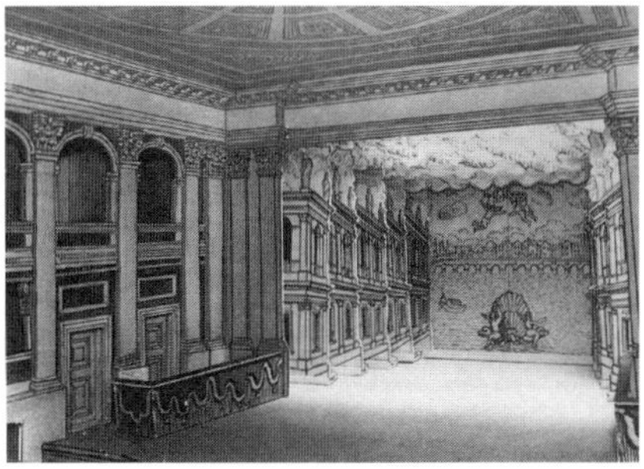

Fig.4 Richard Leacroft, *Reconstruction of the Drury Lane Stage of 1674–1774*

It is not surprising that few managers at this date took their scenery very seriously, as it provided little more than a detached backdrop for the action on the apron stage. It was seldom specially made: the background of Zoffany's *Macbeth* probably depicts one of the theatre's stock scenes – like the 'pair of Gothic wings, very bad and torn' mentioned in the 1776 inventory of the Theatre Royal, Dublin.[23] A later commentator recalled 'the miserable pairs of flats that used to clap together on even the stage trodden by Mr. Garrick; architecture without selection or propriety; a hall, a castle, or a chamber; or a cut of wood of which all the verdure seemed to have been washed away'.[24] All this changed when, during a visit to Paris, Garrick discovered a young French stage-painter called Philippe Jacques de Loutherbourg. He immediately engaged him for Drury Lane, where he served for ten years, transforming theatrical scenery there and making a significant contribution to the history of British landscape painting.[25]

De Loutherbourg's image of Garrick as Don John (No.4) depicts another heroically good-humoured character, this time in an Elizabethan comedy of Beaumont and Fletcher, re-worked by

Garrick in 1754. A lone visitor to Naples, Don John sees an open door late at night and sticks his nose in, looking to help a damsel in distress. A bundle is thrust into his hands, which turns out, when seen in the light, to be a baby. After a career in wenching, Don John reflects, this is a foolish way to acquire a baby; or in his own words, 'am I now bumfiddled with a bastard?' This scene conflates the receiving of the baby from a door and its recognition in the light, again with an expression of dramatic surprise.

The Garrick painting is a cut-down version of a wider composition in the Victoria and Albert Museum, which shows the asymmetrical arrangement of wings to give a natural, picturesque effect, more like a landscape painting than a stage set. De Loutherbourg's other innovations are visible here: a transparent backdrop is lit from behind to create the dramatic moonlight;[26] a vertical column of side-lights (one of Garrick's own inventions) allows for a sudden shaft to fall across Garrick, to accompany his dramatic revelation.[27] No doubt De Loutherbourg is flattering himself, but the lighting here suggests that Garrick is in amongst the scene, rather than acting in front of it. In practice, of course, he would probably have been standing on the apron stage, surrounded by the architecture of the theatre and not the scenery. This would have seemed especially incongruous in the present case, for the gilded doors and boxes of the theatre would have shared the same illusion as the rugged port scene. But things could get worse: the 1773 Bell edition of *Coriolanus* (Act I, scene 1) contains the following surreal stage direction: 'a wood ... Enter at one door Cominus'.[28]

The apron stage shrinks over the period. A visitor to Drury Lane in the early-nineteenth century, after Wyatt's remodelling in 1812, would have seen something resembling a modern stage (Fig.5). The apron stage has been reduced to a tiny strip, flanked by a single diagonal bay, inserted to narrow the proscenium arch so as to keep the size of the stage machinery behind within reasonable limits. These developments give to the proscenium a new importance, for it became, in Wyatt's own words, 'a line of separation between Spectatory and Scene ... to the Scene what the frame of the Picture is to the Picture itself'.[29] Some of the later theatrical paintings in this

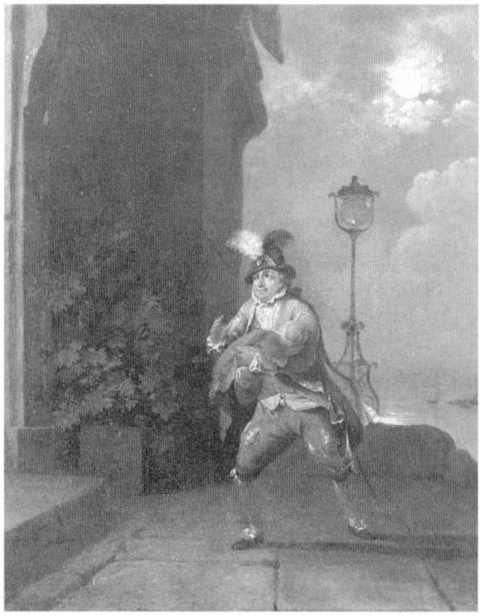

No.4 Philippe Jacques de Loutherbourg
David Garrick as Don John in 'The Chances' by Francis Beaumont and John Fletcher adapted by David Garrick, 1774
Oil on canvas, 35 x 28 cm
The Garrick Club

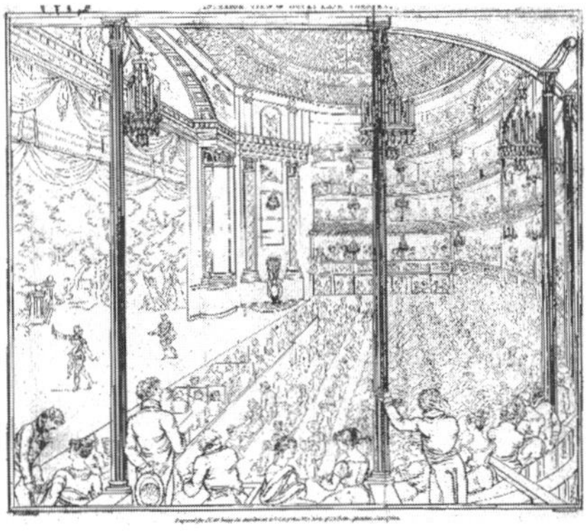

Fig.5 Hopwood, *Interior of Drury Lane Theatre*, 1813
The Theatre Museum, London

exhibition (especially Nos.39 to 41) show figures much more obviously 'framed' by elaborate interiors. They suggest Leigh Hunt's ideal that the scenery of a play should suggest a complete room, 'of which the audience compose the fourth wall'.[30]

It wasn't just the design of the stage area that was changing: theatres were also becoming much bigger during the eighteenth century. The Regency playwright, Richard Cumberland, recalled the days of the old Drury Lane Theatre when, 'as the passions shifted, and were by turns reflected in the mirror of his [Garrick's] expressive countenance, nothing was lost; upon the scale of modern Drury many of the finest touches of his art might necessarily fall short'. For Cumberland Drury Lane and Covent Garden had become 'theatres for spectators rather than playhouses for hearers'.[31] These spectators demanded a new, more projected acting style. This is where the Kembles took the stage.

The Sublime Kembles

Sarah Siddons and her brother, John Philip Kemble made sensational London debuts in 1782 and 1783 respectively. Together they dominated tragic acting for the next thirty years. Comparisons with Garrick, who had recently retired in 1776, were inevitable. Sir Walter Scott sums up the account: Garrick was equally at home in comedy and tragedy; Kemble was humourless; Garrick was short though well-formed, 'Kemble, on the contrary, was tall and stately, his person on a scale suited for the stage and almost too large for a private appartment, with a countenance like the finest models of the antique and motions and manners corresponding to the splendid cast of his form and features'.[32] Kemble's more imposing stage presence made Garrick seem positively homely in retrospect. Zoffany's image of Garrick and Mrs Pritchard (No.2) reminded Kemble of a cook and a butler quarrelling over a kitchen knife.[33] Kemble's more measured style of acting made Garrick seem a fidget.[34]

This may suggest a return to the pre-Garrick years, when larger-than-life actors moved stiffly and declaimed impressively. Various things distinguished the Kembles from the ranting era of James Quin and Colley Cibber. His declamation was more dignified and his acting was more intellectually 'paced'. He built up the dramatic tension slowly and, according to Hazlitt, was capable of 'working up a character from a single "line" of thought or characterisation "and never letting it go"'.[35] It is no accident that Kemble excelled in reflective and introverted parts like Hamlet and Cato. Lawrence's two depictions of Kemble (Nos.5 and 6) are reduced versions of life-sized 'role portraits' (that of Cato painted specially by Lawrence as a gift for his friend Charles Mathews). The originals are ideal conceptions of prince and senator, conceived in the grandest and most universal fashion, rather than records of a specific performance. Both depict the drama of thought, not feeling. Hamlet's macabre banter with a grave-digger has been turned into a celebration of the power of the intellect, which, even from the edge of the grave, can contemplate the stars (No.5). We are reminded of Hamlet's celebration of man – 'In apprehension how like a god!' – rather than his gloomy conclusion, which would have been more appropriate for this setting: 'And yet, to me, what is this quintessence of dust?'.

Above all Kemble made an ideal Roman: heroic, noble and self-controlled. He was sometimes referred to as the 'last of the Romans'.[36] According to Sir Walter Scott, 'other performers might excel Kemble in the full burst of instant and agitating passion ... but we cannot conceive of anyone delineating, with anything approaching the same felicity, those lofty Romans, feeling and partly exhibiting, yet on the whole conquering the passions of nature by the mental discipline to which they had trained themselves'.[37] Addison's *Cato* is the part Scott must have had in mind. Lawrence's portrayal of Kemble in Act V, scene 1 depicts the stiff upper lip of an Augustan Hamlet. As Cato prepares for his suicide, the stage directions read, *'Cato, solus, sitting in a thoughtful posture; in his hand, Plato's book on the Immortality of the Soul. A drawn sword on the table by him'*. Cato is literally being philosophical about his own death. As in Lawrence's depiction of Kemble as Hamlet, the anguish of a doubting mortal is replaced by the exultation of an expanded intellect, contemplating the immortality of the soul, as taught by Plato. Again the effect is

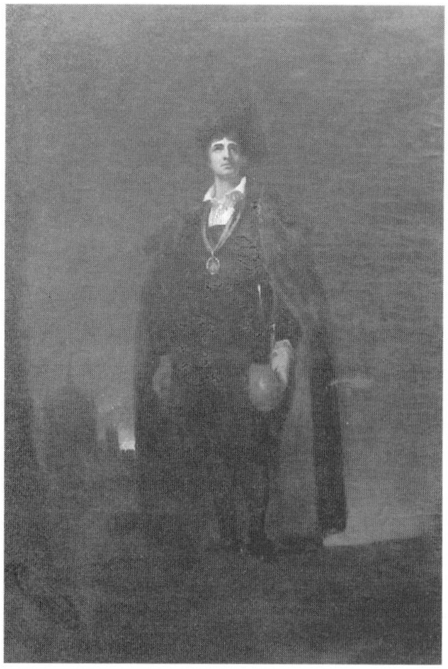

No.5 Sir Thomas Lawrence (studio)
John Philip Kemble as Hamlet
Oil on canvas, 82.6 x 54.6 cm
The Garrick Club

Opposite:
Fig.6 Eagle-Man
From James Carpenter, *Lithographic Drawings Illustrative of the Relation between the Human Physiognomy and that of Brute Creation from designs by Charles Le Brun*, 1827
Cambridge University Library

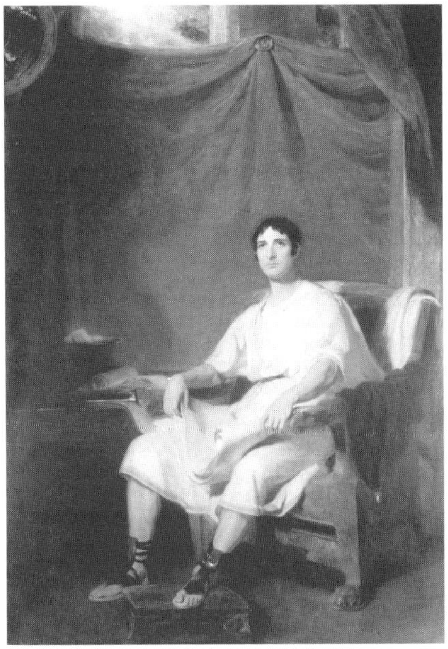

No.6 Sir Thomas Lawrence
John Philip Kemble as Cato in 'Cato' by Joseph Addison
Oil on panel, 109.9 x 73.7 cm
The Garrick Club

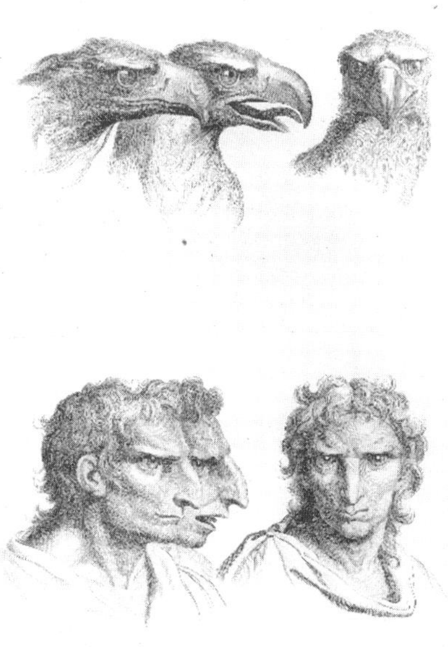

achieved by a transfiguring light, which was doubtless inspired by the lines:

> And yet, methinks, a beam of light breaks in
> On my departing soul (Act V, scene 1).

If Kemble is less shifting in his moods than Garrick, this does not mean that his face is vacant. It is rather expressive at rest, by the very nature of its form, rather than in motion, by the nature of its stimulus. The science which analysed the character of the face was called physiognomy, and it enjoyed a revival at this time following the publication of the first volume of Johan Caspar Lavater's *Physiognomische Fragmente* in 1775. An age-old principle, invented by Aristotle and systematised by Le Brun, says that men have the characters of the species they most resemble (see Fig.6 below). Kemble as Cato is aquiline: he looks like and therefore has the regal character and unblinking gaze of an eagle. In case we miss the reference there is an eagle carved on the arm of his chair. During a row with Sheridan, Kemble is supposed to have bellowed, 'I am an EAGLE, whose wings have been bound down by frosts and snows'.[38] The physiognomic characterisation belongs as much with the part as with the actor: the eagle is the symbol of the Roman Republic, and Cato is the personification of all its virtues. It is Rome itself which is facing death with dignity; as Cato declares (Act II, scene 1), 'My life is grafted on the fate of Rome'.

According to Aristotle, tragedy should inspire Pity and Terror; if Garrick excelled in the former, Kemble and his sister excelled in the latter. In the precise language of the time, they were sublime. Sarah Siddons's performance of the sleep-walking scene in Lady Macbeth (her tour de force) would regularly cause members of the audience to faint away.[39] She introduced a daring innovation: instead of holding a candle, as Mrs Pritchard had, she made as her trademark the wringing of her unencumbered hands.[40] The effect was electrifying: 'It seemed', wrote Hazlitt, 'almost as if a being of a superior order had dropped from a higher sphere to awe the world with the majesty of her appearance ... her gestures were involuntary and mechanical. She

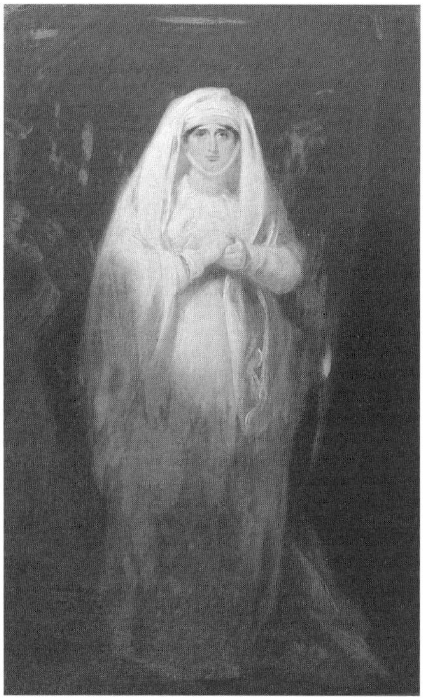

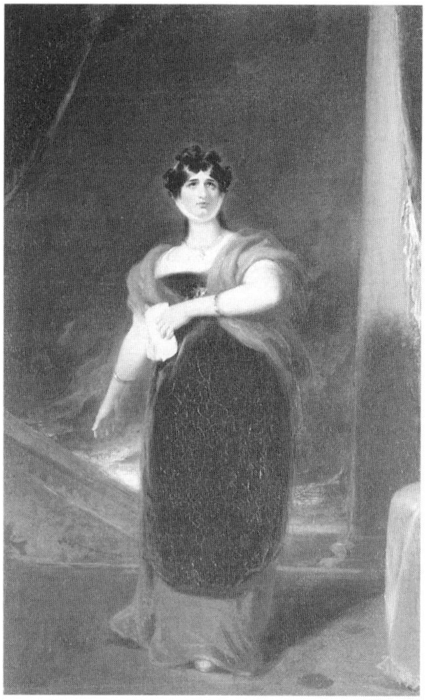

Far left:
No.7 George Henry Harlow
Sarah Siddons as Lady Macbeth, 1814
Oil on canvas, 64 x 39.4 cm
The Garrick Club

Left:
No.8 George Henry Harlow
Sarah Siddons as Lady Macbeth
Oil on canvas, 61 x 38 cm
The Garrick Club

glided on and off the stage like an apparition'.[41] This last sentence describes a peculiar characteristic of both the Kembles – their imposing rigidity. These images of Kemble as Hamlet and Sarah Siddons in the sleep-walking scene (Nos.5 and 7) both have a frontality and a vertical rigidity which is a far cry from conventional deportment, as the contrast in posture between Ross and Kemble (Nos.1 and 5) shows. The Kembles were statuesque: the two factors which, according to James Boaden in 1827, caused Sarah Siddons to change her style were the larger theatres and 'her delight in statuary, which directed her attention to the antique and made a remarkable impression upon her as to simplicity of attire and severity of attitude'.[42] But the examples here have more the sublimity of a primitive standing stone than the grace of a Greek Venus or Apollo. Not everyone was so struck by these unbending postures: Hazlitt thought Kemble was 'the very still life and statuary of the stage ... an icicle upon the bust of tragedy'.[43] Such frigidity was especially absurd off stage: John Philpot Curran (the Irish politician) accused Kemble at

Right:
No.9 Gainsborough Dupont
Joseph George Holman as Edgar in 'King Lear', 1794
Oil on canvas, 73.7 x 62.3 cm
The Garrick Club

Far right:
No.10 Gainsborough Dupont
John Quick as Spado in 'The Castle of Andalusia' by John O'Keeffe, 1794
Oil on canvas, 76 x 63 cm
The Garrick Club

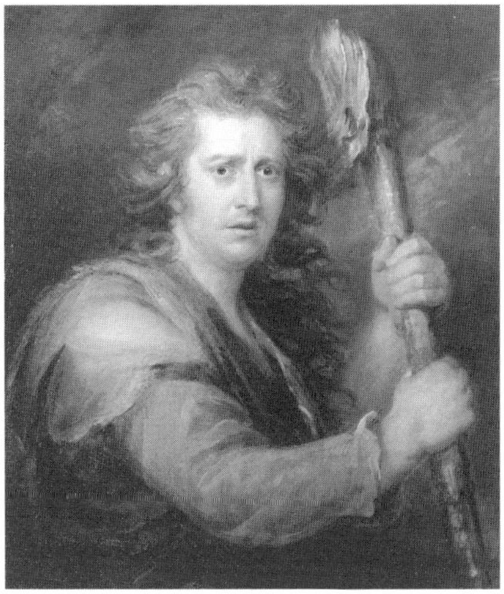

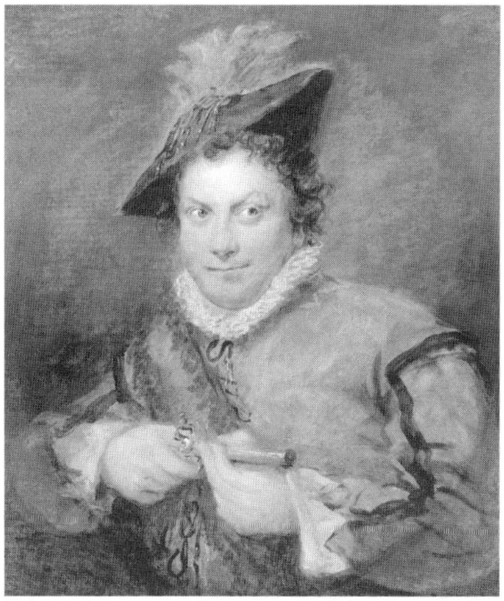

breakfast of looking as if he had eaten a 'poached curtain rod'.[44] Our number 32 (see p.42) shows the comedian Charles Mathews sending up the 'curtain rod' sublimity of Kemble's stage presence.

The styles of Garrick and Kemble cast a long shadow over the eighteenth-century stage. The following two portraits (Nos.9 and 10) are part of a set of the 'principal performers of Covent Garden theatre, in their most distinguished characters', painted by Gainsborough's nephew and assistant Gainsborough Dupont for the manager Thomas Harris.[45] The playwright John O'Keeffe recalls seeing Joseph Holman (1764–1817) posing in the artist's studio, 'on the door of the back drawing-room opening, I was surprised, and a little shocked, to see the room darkened, and lighted by a large lamp hanging from the centre of the ceiling: there stood a man half naked, holding a pole in his stretched-out hand. This was Holman in the character of Edgar, mad Tom'.[46] Dupont has used this atmospheric studio lighting to produce an image saturated with Edgar's wildness and destitution (No.9). The actor supplies the Le Brunian expression of horror; the artist adds some stormy, unkempt hair; a uniform brown tone; and rough handling, which makes the man and his garments seem carved from the same substance as his coarse pole.

John Quick (1748–1831) was the original Tony Lumpkin and a favourite comedian of Covent Garden audiences.[47] Spado, one of a gang of comic-opera bandits, is distinguished by his diminutive stature and insinuating manner. In many ways Dupont's image (No.10) is a comic equivalent of his Edgar: there is the same flicker of the handling to carry the effect of animation in the face across the entire surface of the canvas.

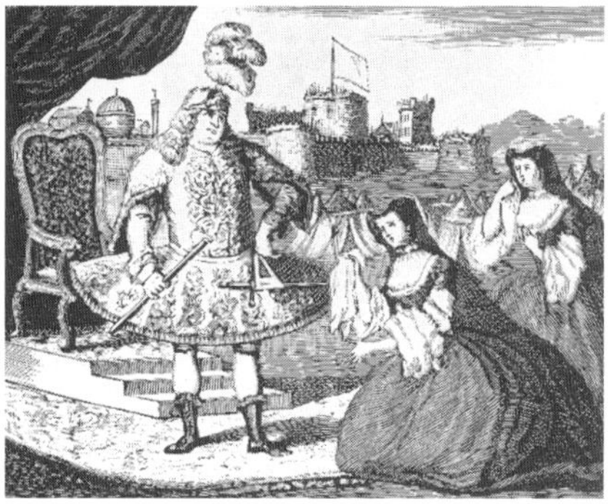

Fig.7 Anonymous caricature of James Quin as Coriolanus, 1749
The Theatre Museum, London

Costume

Writing in 1791, Tate Wilkinson provides a summary of the standard attained in Regency stage costume: 'strict propriety of habiliment not any manager has yet arrived at, even in London ... though it is so highly improved these last twenty years'.[48] It is easy to see this improvement by comparing the Hamlet of David Ross with the Richard III of G.F. Cooke (Nos.1 and 11). Unfortunately such comparisons can be misleading as so much depends not upon the actor but the part. Richard III was historically dressed in Garrick's time. This is because the audience was familiar with the costumes of 'England's Henries and Richards' from 'school and from engravings, medals and firebacks'; they even wore them at masquerades.[49] They are less concerned with Scottish history: Zoffany (No.2) shows Garrick as Macbeth in modern dress (though not the guard's uniform which was the norm). It was not until 1773 that Garrick's rival, Macklin, mounted Macbeth in a version of ancient Scots costume.[50] Suddenly Garrick's coat and waistcoat looked ridiculous: the *St James Chronicle* of 30 October 1773 described him amongst the witches as a 'modern fine gentleman, ... a Beau, who had unfortunately slipped his Foot and tumbled into a Night Cellar, where a Parcel of Old Women were boiling Tripe for their Supper'.[51]

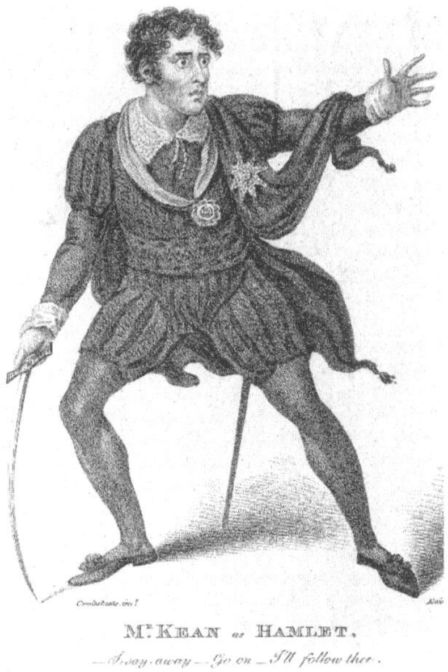

Fig.8 Edmund Kean as Hamlet
The Theatre Museum, London

The first actor-manager to make a conscious policy of historicism was Kemble, who shared with Sir Walter Scott a love of 'dramatic antiquities'.[52] For Kemble, historically accurate sets and costumes contributed to the whole spectacle of a play, along with orchestrated crowd scenes and minor characters learning to act. His Cato is a remarkable advance on previous Roman costume on the eighteenth-century stage. Until his time the Roman 'shape' – a tutu-like version

Opposite:
Fig.10 Charles Macklin as Shylock in *The Merchant of Venice*, 1775
The Theatre Museum, London

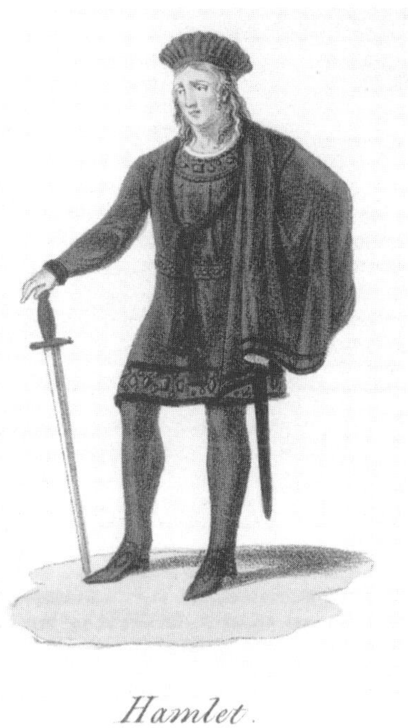

Fig.9 Plate from J.R. Planché, *Illustrated Guide to the Dress of Shakespeare's Plays*, 1850

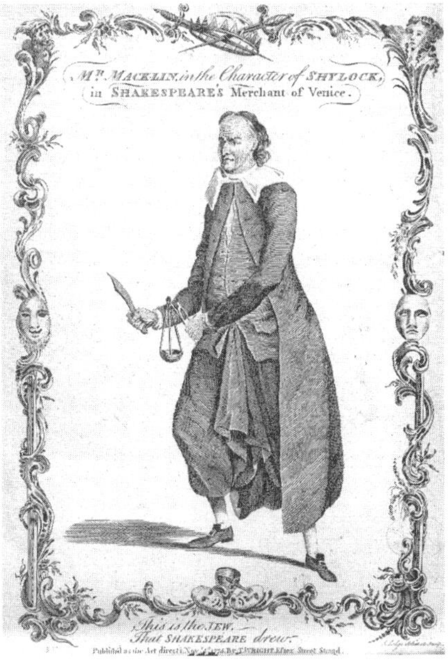

of Roman armour (Fig.7) – was worn for all ancient men, whether or not they were soldiers, often playing opposite women in contemporary ball-gowns.[53] Cato wears an authentic Roman tunic, the garment worn underneath a toga in public and on its own in private.

There was still a long way to go in historical costume, especially in those parts, chief amongst them being Hamlet, where the historical reality seemed remote and irrelevant. Our exhibition shows two modern-dress Hamlets of c.1760 (Nos.1 and 35): Garrick was still in coat and waistcoat for the part in the 1770s. Kemble's Hamlet (No.5) shows him in Elizabethan dress adjusted to resemble the timeless black cloak of a melancholy scholar. Edmund Kean's Hamlet (Fig.8) is a more accurate and intricate version of Elizabethan dress. Even this development left room for real historical research, which was supplied by the playwright and manager, James Robinson Planché. According to him 'the alterations made in the costume of the plays founded upon English history in particular, while they rendered them more picturesque, added but little to their propriety; the whole series, King Lear included, being dressed in the habits of the Elizabethan era ... and, strictly speaking, very inaccurately representing the costume even of that period'.[54] With this in mind Planché set about educating his audience from scratch with a series of illustrated guides to the dress of Shakespeare's plays, the first of which, *Dramatic Costume: Costume of Shakespeare's Historical Tragedy of King John*, came out in 1823.[55] Planché collaborated with Kemble's younger brother Charles on a simultaneous production of *King John*, with historically accurate costumes, which 'initiated a new departure in theatrical art'.[56] Other plays were to follow, including *Hamlet*, where the prince appeared sporting a specially designed and suitably bizarre-looking habit (Fig.9).

Shylock and Richard III, the two parts played here by G.F. Cooke (Nos.11 and 12), were the earliest to be authentically dressed when Garrick and Macklin took them in 1741 (Fig.10). Cooke's Shylock is clearly influenced by Macklin's in scornful expression as well as costume, just as his Richard was inspired by Garrick's. But both dresses are overlaid with trimmings and costume jewellery to give them an exotic brilliance, which is expressive if not authentic.

The Romantics: George Frederick Cooke and Edmund Kean

G. F. Cooke (1756–1812) was an exact contemporary of J. P. Kemble. But having spent most of his career touring the provinces, his sensational debut as Richard III and subsequent brief London career (1800–10) seemed to offer the capital a new acting style. It is for this reason that he can be bracketed with the much younger Edmund Kean (1789–1833), who made his London debut as Shylock in 1814 and whose meteoric career was effectively burnt out by 1825. It was as Richard and Shylock that Garrick and Macklin launched themselves; it was in the same parts that Cooke and Kean defined their identity in contrast to the Kembles. Both their repertoires were made up of such outcasts and tortured villains: Cooke also specialised in Richard II, Iago, Kitely, Macbeth and Sir Giles Overreach; Kean in Othello, Hamlet and Iago.

Neither Shylock nor Richard III were ever Kemble's strong parts (Walter Scott recalls how he 'could never look the part of Richard'); he was evidently content to leave them to Cooke.[57] One Jean Genest, writing in 1832, compared the two actors: 'Cooke did not possess that elegant figure of Kemble, but his countenance beamed with great intelligence – his eyes were fiery, dark, and at times terribly expressive, particularly in the worst passions of our nature ... his attitudes [were] less picturesque that Kemble's ... but they were just, appropriate and natural'; Kemble excelled as Coriolanus and Hamlet; Cooke as Richard III, where his figure was good, 'his face better, his voice better, his habitual manner better, as being more quick, abrupt and impetuous'.[58] Another critic felt that Cooke's Richard was 'somewhat deficient in the kingly and heroic part', but shone in 'all the subtle, ludicrous, sarcastic turns of the character ... We have seen Richard rendered more awful and terrific, but never more thoroughly detestable ... His delivery of the passage ... "Why I can smile and murder while I smile" ... conveyed the idea of a man, sensible of his personal deformities and the barriers which separated him from the rest of his brethren, hugging himself up and enjoying a horrible satisfaction in the possession of a faculty by which he hoped to overreach the rest of mankind and secure the grand object of his eye'.[59]

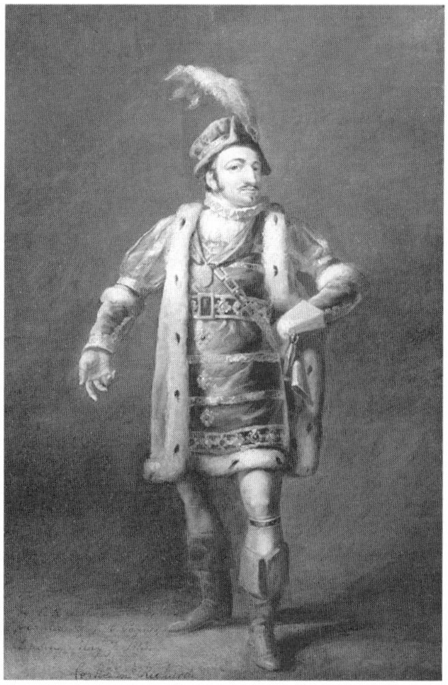

No.11 Charles Robert Leslie
George Frederick Cooke as Richard III,
1813
Oil on canvas, 44.5 x 29.2 cm
The Garrick Club

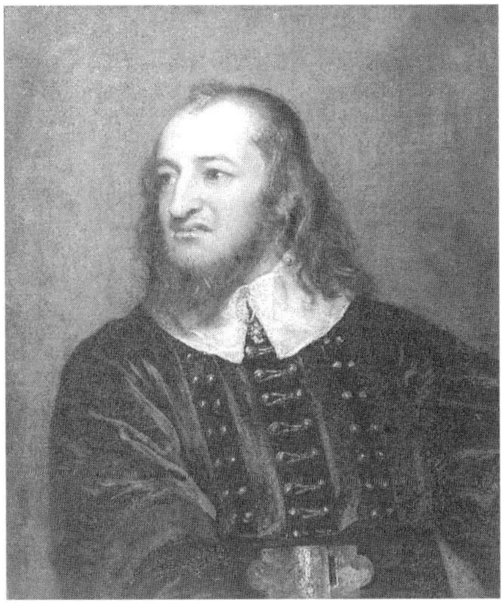

No.12 Thomas Phillips
George Frederick Cooke as Shylock in 'The Merchant of Venice', 1803
Oil on canvas, 76 x 63 cm
The Garrick Club

Charles Leslie's small portrait of Cooke as Richard III (No.11) brings these descriptions to life. Richard is clearly delivering a soliloquy (perhaps even the one mentioned above); unlike Kemble's Hamlet, Cooke actually addresses the audience, with an insinuating directness which was usually reserved for comedy. He bows to us in a reasonably graceful posture, though his deformity is hinted at in the unusual twist of his right arm. This might seem at least a courtly, if not kingly, act of courtesy, except that the bow is so sarcastic, so exaggerated in its mock obsequiousness. It is as if he cannot conceal his contempt for the objects of his dissimulation. He is indeed 'hugging himself up and enjoying a horrible satisfaction' in the possession of his satanic cunning.

Cooke's Shylock (No.12) is a snap-shot of scorn. Phillips seems to have painted the expression from Le Brun's illustration of that emotion, with flashing eyes, swivelled head, turned-down mouth and bared teeth. With his whispy beard, receding yet long hair and exotic costume, Cooke makes of Shylock a terrifying outcast. Depictions of Garrick in villainous roles show a handsome man playing a monster. Cooke wasn't so handsome: according to a contemporary, 'his features are thoughtful, bold and marked, and calculated to give the expression of scorn, envy, hatred, brutal ferocity and overbearing pride with unrivalled force and effect'.[60] He isn't here playing a monster; he has become one.

Edmund Kean is probably the most vividly described actor in history. For Coleridge his acting was 'like reading Shakespeare by flashes of lightning'.[61] For Hazlitt it was 'like an anarchy of the passions, in which each upstart humour, or frenzy of the moment, is struggling to get violent possession of some bit or corner of his fiery soul and pygmy body – to jostle out and lord it over the rest of the rabble of short-lived and furious passions'.[62]

Clint's little oil sketch (No.13) perfectly conveys the 'fiery soul' twisting the 'pygmy body' into a contortion of passion. Kean was clearly less dignified and more natural than Kemble: Hazlitt recalls, 'we used to admire Mr Kemble's figure and manner, and had no idea that there was any want of art or nature. We feel the force and nature of Mr Kean's acting, but then we feel the want of Mr Kean's person'.[63]

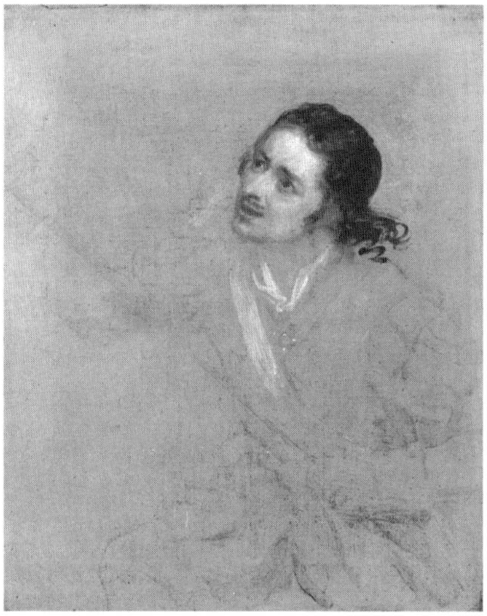

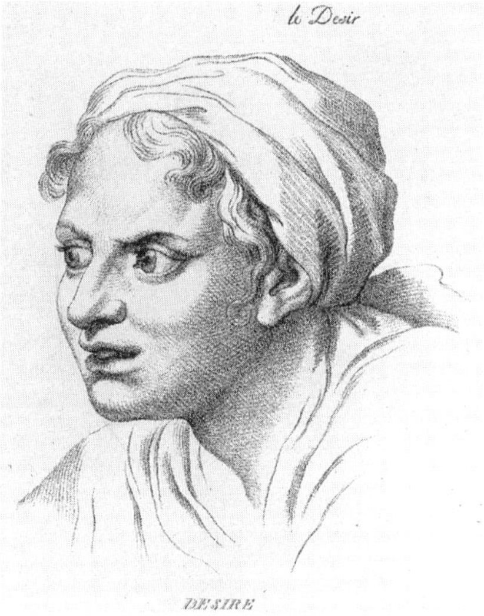

Far left:
No.13 George Clint
Edmund Kean as Richard III
Oil on canvas, 52.5 x 41.3 cm
The Garrick Club

Left:
Fig.11 Desire
Plate from Bowles's *Passions of the Soul, from the Designs of the late Celebrated Monsieur Le Brun*, 1780s
Cambridge University Library

Another reviewer felt that he was so 'matter of fact' that he was like a 'poet who disdains metaphor'.[64] Kean's Richard here is not just matter of fact, he is mean, insinuating, even cringing. At first sight one might assume Richard is drawing his sword to perpetrate some crime, which would at least have some heroism to it. In fact he is playing his most abject role in the play – the improbable lover. He kneels to Lady Anne, whose husband he has murdered, and offers his sword and naked breast:

> Lo! here I lend thee this sharp-pointed sword;
> Which if thou please to hide in this true breast,
> And let the soul forth that adoreth thee
> (Act 1, scene 2).

For all his 'anarchy of passions' Kean's acting and Clint's painting are still subject to expressive systems: Kean here clearly wears the expression of 'Desire', as recommended by Le Brun (Fig.11). This is the appropriate expression for his situation, though an extra tilt of the head takes away the dignity of the Le Brun and suggests the fawning of an otherwise vicious dog.

Comedy of Manners

In the course of a letter to the comedian Charles Mathews, dated 30 May 1814, Samuel Taylor Coleridge offered a definition of comedy: 'that which gives us the passions of men, and their endless modifications and influences, or thoughts, gestures, &c., modified in their turn by circumstances of rank, relations, nationality, &c., instead of mere transitory manners; in short, the inmost man represented on the superficies, instead of the superficies merely representing itself'.[65] These priorities are familiar to us from tragedy, particularly the idea that the theatre is a profound inquiry into the operations of the now familiar 'passions'. Sir Walter Scott expressed himself in a similar vein when he complained that the majority pronounced Charles Mathews a mimic, when they ought to have considered him 'an accurate and philosophic observer of human nature, blessed with a rare talent for intuitively identifying himself with the minds of others'.[66] The difference between comedy and tragedy lies in Coleridge's modifications by 'circumstances of rank, relations, nationality, &c.'. Tragedy is universal; comedy is 'modified'. The time and place of comedy matters. The vast majority of comedies in the eighteenth century dealt with modern life, while those set in the past deliberately allowed a modern colouring to the characterisation. So it is that the images in this section work as a satirical commentary on the fashionable vices and follies of eighteenth-century society in much the same way that Hogarth's prints do.

Clearly there is some contradiction between these particulars and the generalising power of the 'philosophical' comedian, admired by Coleridge and Scott. In fact almost all comic characters in the period, even if based on particular people, are stock types identified by a descriptive 'character-label' – Sir Archy Macsarcasm, Snarl, Flexible, etc. These types can in their turn be arranged into broader stock-categories. When Mathews claimed that he could do the 'entire range of low comedy', the manager of Covent Garden, George Colman, wanted to know 'in which part of that range you feel yourself to have succeeded most with the audience. Old men, country boys, dapper servants, ... &c'.[67] One begins to suspect that, for the eighteenth century, just as there were ten passions, so there were ten types of comic character.

Clowns and Rustics

We have already seen that a tragedian's posture is founded upon the habits of eighteenth-century high society, and yet its function is to suggest 'timeless' dignity. Society's habits have more importance in comedy – they are its very substance – and yet they function differently. Correct deportment in a comedy draws attention to itself: it reminds you of the rank of the character and serves to distinguish him from others; it is informative. Hogarth wrote that a foreigner could visit an English theatre and know everything about the characters, especially about their class, from the way they stood, without understanding a word they said. Lichtenberg shows how this might be done, when he describes an encounter between gentleman and servant in Farquhar's *Beaux' Stratagem.* Archer (played by Garrick) is a nobleman pretending to be a servant; Scrub (played by Weston) is a real servant who tries to ape his new colleague's 'ease of demeanour' and comes hopelessly unstuck. That 'ease of demeanour', which would be treated as a matter of course in Garrick's performance of Hamlet, becomes comically picked over, movement by movement, in his performance of Archer.[68]

As the example of Garrick reminds us, an actor, unless specifically required by a part to do otherwise, should stand and speak as gracefully as possible. Thomas King as Touchstone is quite as elegant as any Hamlet (No.14). This is because in poetic Shakespearean comedy even the clown is gentrified; in just the same way that his costume is a fanciful eighteenth-century version of motley, often worn to fashionable masquerades. Touchstone represents the court (in contrast to the rustic, Corin); at this moment he is declaiming. This painting may have been cut down to remove a Rosalind from the left-hand side, towards whom Touchstone is addressing his mock love poetry:

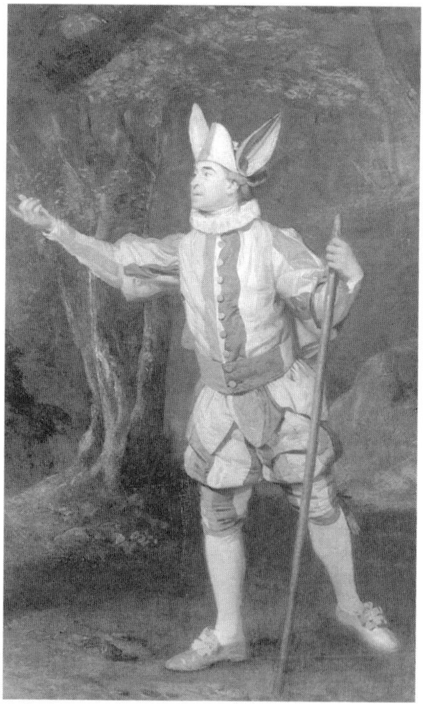

No.14 Johan Zoffany
Thomas King as Touchstone in 'As You Like It', c.1770
Oil on canvas, 91 x 55.5 cm
The Garrick Club

Opposite:
No.16 Samuel De Wilde
John Bannister as Scout and William Parsons as Snarl in 'The Village Lawyer'
c.1787
Oil on canvas, 92 x 71.5 cm
The Garrick Club

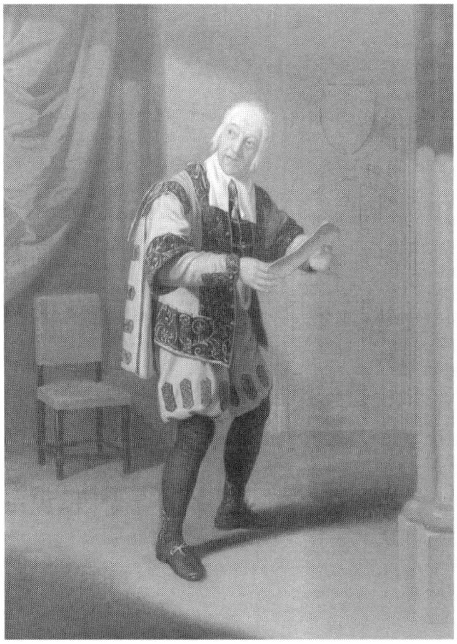

No.15 Samuel De Wilde
Joseph Munden as Verdun in 'Lovers' Vows' by Elizabeth Inchbald, 1799
Oil on canvas, 73.7 x 55.9 cm
The Garrick Club

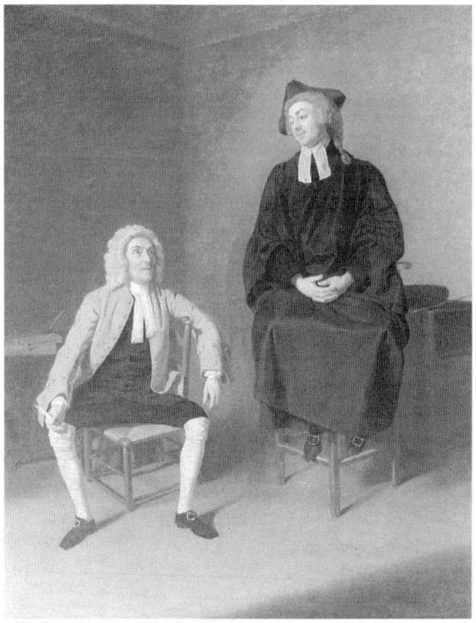

If a hart do lack a hind,
Let him seek out Rosalind, etc.
(Act III, scene 2).

The grace of the posture here may then be an ironic flourish or merely the declaiming style of an actor who was a well-loved exponent of the 'old school of acting'.[69] Thomas King (1730–1805) was Garrick's discovery and eventual replacement (from 1764 to 1788) as the principal Drury Lane comedian, during which time he created the part of Lord Ogleby (see No.38) in 1766 and played Touchstone on numerous occasions after his debut in the part in 1767.

Touchstone makes a striking contrast with another rhyming servant, Verdun, in Elizabeth Inchbald's *Lover's Vows* (No.15). The play – the one that caused all the fuss in Jane Austen's *Mansfield Park* – is an adaptation of the German playwright Kotzebue, who was enormously and unaccountably popular at the time. Verdun adds a touch of leaden-handed comedy to the gross sentimentality of the main plot. He is a garrulous poetaster (his name probably intended to suggest *Vers d'un*), a kind of stage MacGonogal anxious to read his doggerel verses at any provocation. Verdun is obviously declaiming and no doubt wanting to look like Touchstone, but Munden's stooping shoulders, bent knees and shifty, side-long glance announce the comical stage-plebeian. His elaborate, slightly Elizabethan, costume and Gothic setting are intended to convey a vague idea of 'olde merrie Germanie'. Joseph Munden (1758–1832, see also No.39) apparently excelled in this sort of character, mingling 'sentiment and fun'.[70] It is probably no accident that there is a Hogarthian broadness to the characterisation: Charles Lamb wrote of Munden, 'in what has been truly denominated the "sublime of farce" Munden stands out as single and unaccompanied as Hogarth'.[71]

Another of Garrick's discoveries, who dominated the Drury Lane stage from 1778 until his retirement in 1815, was John Bannister (1760–1836). The three images of Bannister in this exhibition (Nos.16, 17 and 18) are unusually complex, which probably owes something to the actor as well as to the artist. Bannister trained as a painter with De Loutherbourg (see No.4) and was a friend of the prominent artists of the day, as well as the actors and writers. The two parts here show his particular aptitude for extracting comedy from plausible and buoyant (if rather feckless) young gentlemen. Lawyers were favourite comic characters with all actors, partly because they made up such a large proportion of the audience. Their stage quality is a cheerful sort of bare-faced knavery – an ability to argue that black is white.

The first two paintings illustrate *The Village Lawyer*, a farce translated from the French by one Mr Lyons. The first (No.16) shows a contest between a mean and cheating tailor (Snarl) and the impoverished village lawyer of the title. Scout means to 'hum him out of a suit' (pun absolutely intended), in the case of 'Lawyer *versus* Tailor – suit for the Plaintiff, damages for the Defendant'. Scout gets his cloth by the classic con-man's routine of promising £50 to take possession of £5. The legal and adversarial language elevates a scam to an encounter of wits. Hence the simplified and strikingly symmetrical image. The lawyer sits on the tailor's high stool in front of the cloth which he has finessed. The tailor sits on a low chair, with a quill and a table of books – he is left with empty words, the lawyer's wares. The absurd difference in the chair height conveys Scout's grand condescension, which has so dazzled Snarl; it also makes manifest the simple idea of a see-saw, with lawyer in the ascendant.

Bannister's cheerfully benign expression turns to comic outrage during his next encounter, at which he is outwitted by a peasant (No.17). Sheepface has got off a sheep-stealing charge by simulating idiocy aggravated by brain damage: at Scout's suggestion, he has answered all the judge's questions by bleating like a sheep. Scout demands his fee and receives the same unhelpful response. Again we see an adversarial encounter, this time between bookish and illiterate cunning. The contrast between the two contestants is entirely conveyed by the comedy of deportment. It all hangs on the feet: for the guiding rule of gentlemanly deportment, seen in Nivelon's *The Rudiments of Genteel Behaviour* (Fig.1, see p.9), is that the feet should be places at right angles to each other. Bannister's elegantly thrown-back head and shoulders rest upon this secure basis. Parson's feet are resolutely parallel, conveying an odious slouch up through the bent knees and slumped shoulders.

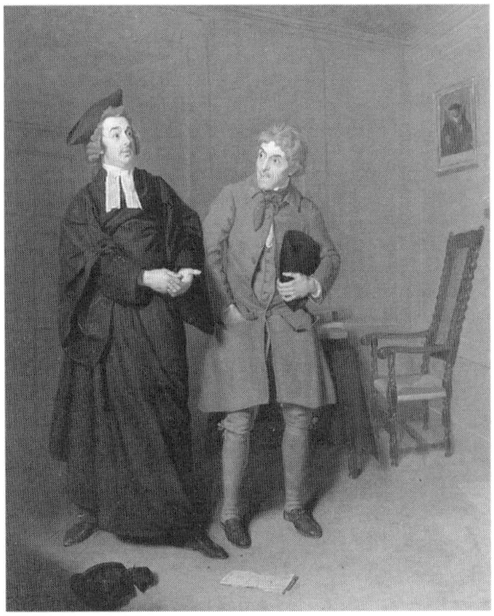

No.17 Samuel De Wilde
John Bannister as Scout and William Parsons as Sheepface in 'The Village Lawyer', 1793
Oil on canvas, 77 x 63 cm
The Garrick Club

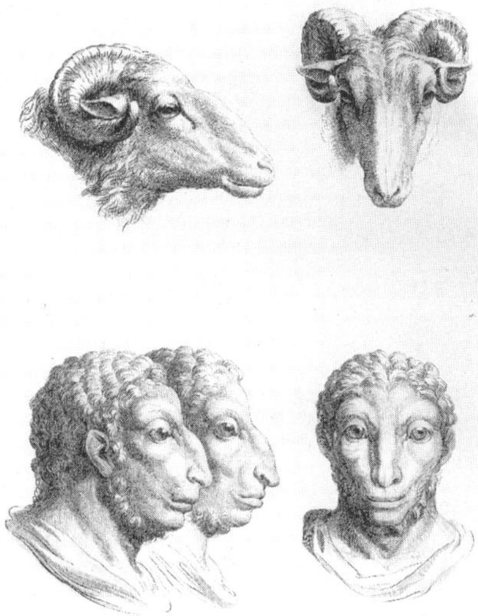

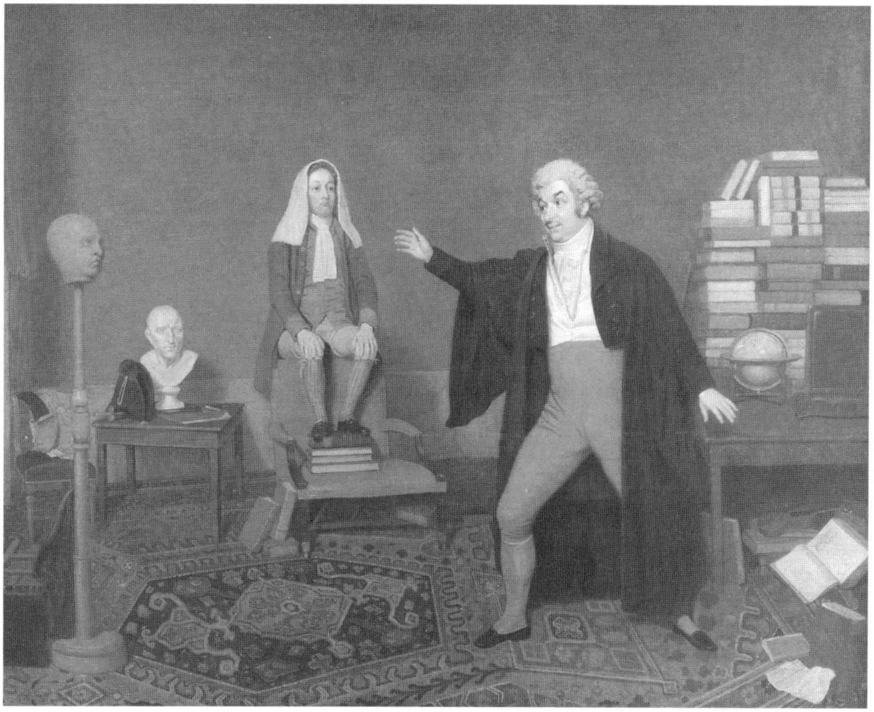

No.18 Samuel De Wilde
John Bannister as Tristram Fickle and John Purser as Sneer in 'The Weathercock' by John Till Allingham, 1808
Oil on canvas, 101.6 x 121.9 cm
The Garrick Club

According to his biographer, Bannister 'exercised his talents in a display of the heads by which Lavater illustrated his system of physiognomy'.[72] The most popular 'system of physiognomy' was the one, mentioned above, which gives to men the characters of the animals they resemble. According to this system, Sheepface is clearly ovine. Figure 12 shows Ram-Man from a series of lithographs illustrating Le Brun's system of physiognomy, published in 1827. Sheepface has the same protruding muzzle, humped-back nose, splayed and bulging eyes, and stubble hair; in short he has the face and the character of a sheep.

The science of physiognomy is also strongly suggested by De Wilde's final rendering of John Bannister (No.18), this time in *The Weathercock*. Tristram Fickle is not actually a lawyer, he is just trying on the profession for size. He is the 'weathercock' of the title – a feckless young gentleman, unable to settle upon any fixed form of employment. At this moment he is a passionate advocate, pleading against a wig-stand in front of a judge, impersonated by his servant, Sneer.

Opposite:
Fig.12 Ram-Man
From James Carpenter, *Lithographic Drawings Illustrative of the Relation between the Human Physiognomy and that of Brute Creation from designs by Charles Le Brun*, 1827
Cambridge University Library

Soon his enthusiasm will transfer to another profession. His Fickle nature is expressed through the jumble of books and instruments which crowd his study, suggesting an encyclopaedic knowledge comically at variance with his cheerfully vacant expression. The bust of Cicero and the unused wig-stand both resemble those bald demonstration heads, marked-up by phrenologists. This spurious air of physiognomic science draws attention to the absurd contrast between the two living characters – the ebullient Tristram and the acidic Sneer, one of Nature's hanging judges.

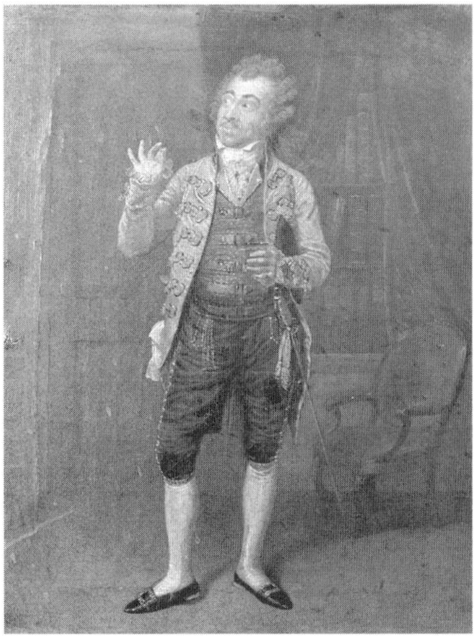

No.19 Samuel De Wilde
Samuel Simmons as Beau Mordecai in 'Love à la Mode' by Charles Macklin
c.1800
Oil on canvas, 36.5 x 28 cm
The Garrick Club

The Bourgeois Gentleman

Molière's play of this name (1670) is the most famous and influential example of a stock comic formula – the man who tries too hard. Shoals of eighteenth-century characters are built upon this simple idea. It usually happens with outsiders trying to get in. For example, no expense or effort could reverse the misfortune of being born a tradesman or a foreigner. Parvenus or nouveaux riches were usually called 'cits' in the eighteenth century, on the assumption that they made their money in the city. When they decided to set up as country gentlemen they could be relied upon to overshoot. Foreigners are obviously affected and over-dressed; their ways can even infect good English gentlemen, turning them into ridiculous fops. Lord Chesterfield explains how to spot them: 'the difference in this case between a man of sense and a fop, is, that the fop values himself upon his dress, and the man of sense laughs at it, at the same time that he knows he must not neglect it'.[73] This is evidently a fine line, which has been crossed in different ways by this small group of stage fashion-victims (Nos.19–23).

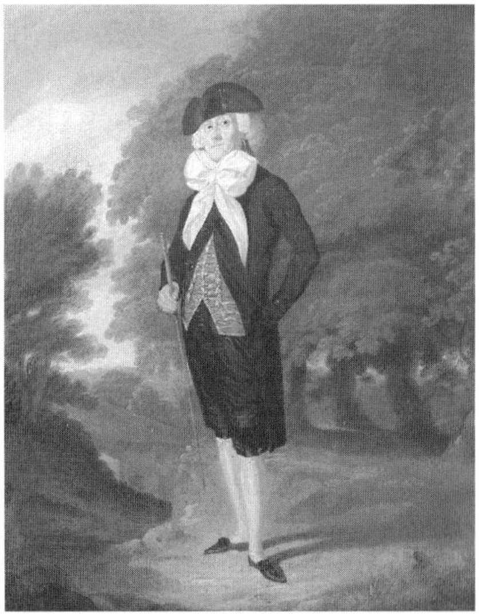

As a cit and a Jew, Beau Mordecai (No.19) is doubly excluded from the fashionable world; yet 'in spite of nature and education, [he] sets up for a wit, a gentleman, and a man of taste' (Act I, scene 1). Not surprisingly he comes unstuck: he is described by his dour rival, Archy Macsarcasm, as a 'fantastical baboon'. He is 'trick'd out in all the colours of the rainbow'; his posture betrays the prance of the

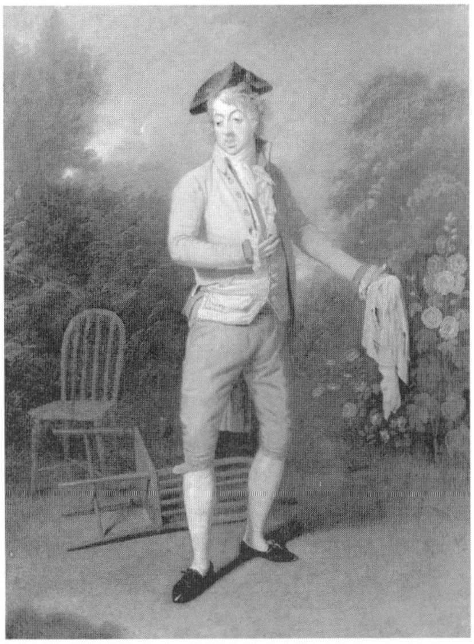

No.21 Samuel De Wilde
Robert Palmer as Tag in 'The Spoiled Child' by Isaac Bickerstaffe, 1797
Oil on canvas, 77.3 x 59.3 cm
The Garrick Club

Opposite:
No.20 Samuel De Wilde
Richard Suett as Endless in 'No Song, No Supper' by Prince Hoare, c.1790
Oil on canvas, 43.9 x 34.3 cm
The Garrick Club

dancing master; his snuff-taking is a pantomime; and his witty expression is an absurd grimace. His physiognomy is literally simian, a racist comparison between monkey and Jew also drawn by Hogarth in scene 2 of *The Harlot's Progress.*

Endless (No.20) is a bent lawyer courting a farmer's wife as part of a plot to have him evicted. He is dressed for the kill: 'this dress', he opines, 'cannot fail of captivating Dorothea's heart'.[74] He is a walking parody of the 'macaronis', as the fops of the 1790s were called. They wore just this type of puffed-out cravat and starved themselves to a fashionable thinness. Urban over-dressing of this kind appears especially ludicrous in the middle of a wood. Richard Suett (1755–1805) was himself unusually tall and thin and exploited his physique for comic effect. Charles Lamb wrote that 'Shakespeare foresaw him when he framed his fools and jesters. They have all the true Suett stamp – a loose and shambling gait, a slippery tongue'.[75]

Tag (No.21) is another type of not-quite-gentleman: a poor actor with nothing to recommend him except the effrontery of the stage. He is seeking to elope with a rich old maid called Miss Pickle. However, during their secret meeting in the garden, the 'spoiled child' of the title – a boy called Little Pickle, often played by Mrs Jordan – sews their clothes together. In this image they have just sprung apart, overturning one of the chairs, while Tag tries to regain his gallant composure with a bow, the torn fragment of his coat held like a handkerchief.

It is hard to tell which of the many versions of *The Marriage of Figaro* produced in England during the Regency period is illustrated here (No.22). The music was probably Mozart's, but it would have been performed in English with spoken dialogue by repertory actors and actresses. *The Cabinet* (No.23) was also an opera, though the composer of the music is not recorded.

The comparison between these two small images gives a new twist to the contrast between fop and man of sense. As his name suggests, the Marquis de Grand Château (No.23) is a typical French grandee of ludicrous pomp and vanity, who is imposed upon the heroine of the piece as an advantageous match. He enters followed by six gentlemen in 'splendid liveries'; he speaks with 'affected gallantry . . . vainly

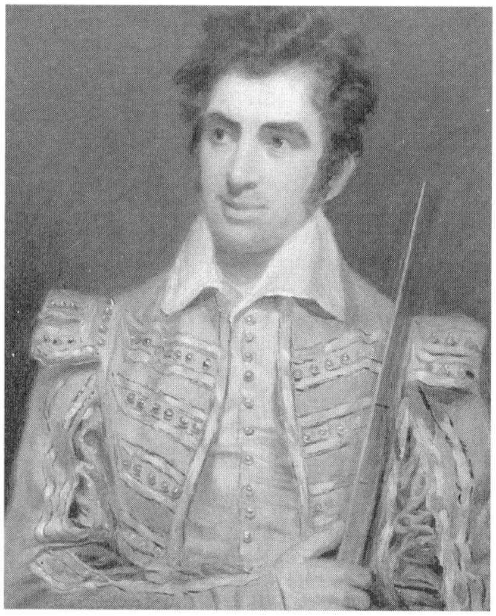

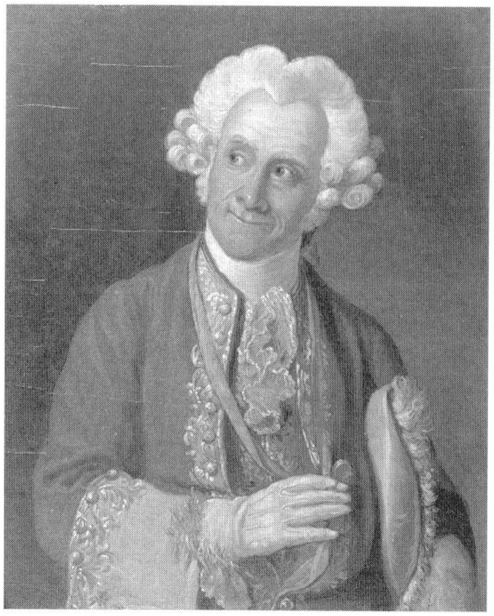

Far left:
No.22 George Clint
Vincent Decamp as Figaro in 'Follies of a Day or the Marriage of Figaro' by Thomas Holcroft
Oil on panel, 29.2 x 24.1 cm
The Garrick Club

Left:
No.23 Samuel De Wilde
William Blanchard as the Marquis de Grand Château in 'The Cabinet' by Thomas John Dibdin
Oil on panel, 25.3 x 20.8 cm
The Garrick Club

struggling to conceal his age and infirmities'; he even gets his 'ideas of rational affection, and connubial happiness' drafted by his flunky, Manikin. Figaro is also a flunky, but he is no manikin. In Clint's painting he appears young, alert, handsome and elegant – a man of sense in fact; in contrast to the Marquis who is a leering, wrinkled, powdered and antiquated fop.

Ladies

> The pompous train, the swelling phrase, and the unnatural rant are displaced for that natural portrait of human folly and frailty, of which all are judges, because all have sat for the picture
>
> Goldsmith, *An Essay on the Theatre*, 1772.[76]

The characters mentioned above clearly satisfy Goldsmith's criterion: they are 'natural portraits' of 'human folly and frailty'. His remarks draw attention to two things constantly repeated about comedy, especially in the latter part of the century. Comedy should be a portrait of the audience and it should be improving. In 1747 Garrick spoke a prologue, written by Samuel Johnson, to celebrate the re-opening of the Drury Lane theatre. In it he referred to the Restoration stage when,

> Themselves they studied, as they felt they writ,
> Intrigue was Plot, Obscenity was Wit.
> Vice always found a sympathetic Friend;
> They pleas'd their Age, and did not aim to mend.

Garrick on the other hand aimed to please and mend with what Johnson calls 'useful Mirth'. It was later claimed that 'since Mr. Garrick's Management, the Stage is become the School of Manners and Morality ... the British can now vie with the Athenian Drama, when in its Severest State of Purity'.[77]

For a variety of reasons the moral side of social commentary is more in evidence in the treatment of women than of men. The images in this section show how women should and should not be. The criteria are similar to those for men except that with women the heart is more important that the head: so that the equivalent ideal to the 'man of sense' is a 'woman of feeling'.

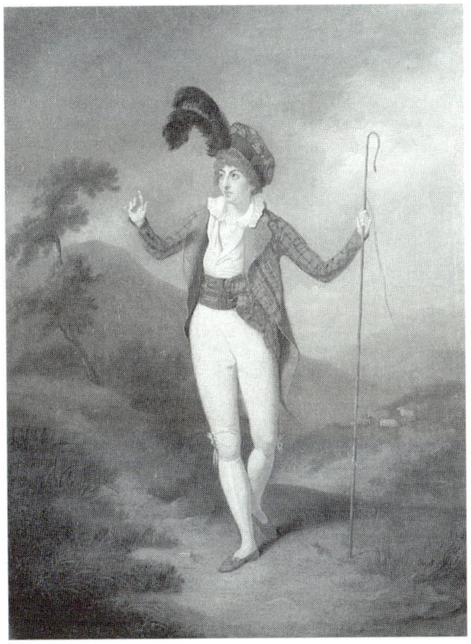

No.24 Samuel De Wilde
Maria Theresa Kemble as Patie in 'The Gentle Shepherd' by Allan Ramsay, adapted by Richard Tickell, c.1796
Oil on canvas, 74.3 x 53.3 cm
The Garrick Club

It is perhaps surprising that one of the most ideal images of women in this section should be that of Mrs Kemble playing a man (No.24). Allan Ramsay's pastoral poem *The Gentle Shepherd*, was first written in 1725, but became an ideal vehicle for the sentimental worship of simple nature advocated by Jean-Jacques Rousseau and his followers in the last quarter of the century. This operatic adaptation (first performed in 1781) was the work of two men familiar from Dulwich Picture Gallery's permanent collection: Richard Tickell, husband of Mary Linley (seen in Gainsborough's portrait of *The Linley Sisters*, DPG320) wrote the words and Thomas Linley (seen again in a Gainsborough portrait, DPG331) wrote the music. Maria Theresa Decamp was Vincent's sister (see No.22) and Charles Kemble's wife (see No.41); she first took the part of Patie, the gentle shepherd of the title, in 1796.

This is what is called a 'breeches part', a type invented in 1699 when Peg Woffington played Sir Harry Wildair in Farquhar's *The Constant Couple*. This excuse to parade women's legs in public sounds like a hang-over from the age when 'obscenity was wit'. It was lampooned as such in a print of 1779 entitled *Miss Brazen just Breecht*. But Maria Kemble doesn't really look a Miss Brazen: her dress seems more intended to display that grace of posture which belongs with the unaffected child of nature. According to a contemporary reviewer, the characters were dressed 'with rustic simplicity, which tho' not exactly characteristic of the Highland manner, were perfectly Pastoral'.[78]

Mrs Abington (No.25) is one of a handful of actresses whose success spilled over from the stage into society. She became an arbiter of fashion in a way that no male star ever did. A theatrical historian of the day recalls that 'in addition to the grace, the ease, and the elegance with which Mrs Abington personated characters in high life ... her taste for dress was novel and interesting. She was consulted by fine ladies of the first distinction ... from a decided conviction of her judgement in blending what was beautiful with what was becoming. Indeed, dress took a sort of *ton* from her fancy'.[79] Real life and the stage are further confused in Hickey's portrait of Mrs Abington in *The Maid of the Oaks*. The 'Oaks' was a real place – the seat of Lord Stanley – which in 1774 was given over to a *fête champêtre* to celebrate his marriage to Lady Betty Hamilton.[80] It was at this fanciful party that General Burgoyne's play (about a *fête champêtre* to celebrate a wedding) was first performed. So the play is a party within a party. The fancy-dress costume in Hickey's painting and the idyllic setting – a summer's evening among the garden temples – recall the circumstances of real life as well as stage. Indeed very similar devices are used for 'ordinary' portraits of this date, like Gainsborough's *Mrs Graham* of 1777 (National Gallery of Scotland). These things would suggest that Lady Bab is such as might walk out of a Watteau painting: romantic, poetical and in tune with flowers. In fact she is a 'princess of dissipation' who is as uneasy in the country as a 'mole in sunshine'.[81] This image is thus ambiguously poised between being a celebration of a woman's romantic sensibility and the depiction of a brilliant actress playing a flirt.

A very similar ambiguity occurs with Singleton's portrait of Maria Davison (No.26). She is clearly dazzling and beautiful, but that is just

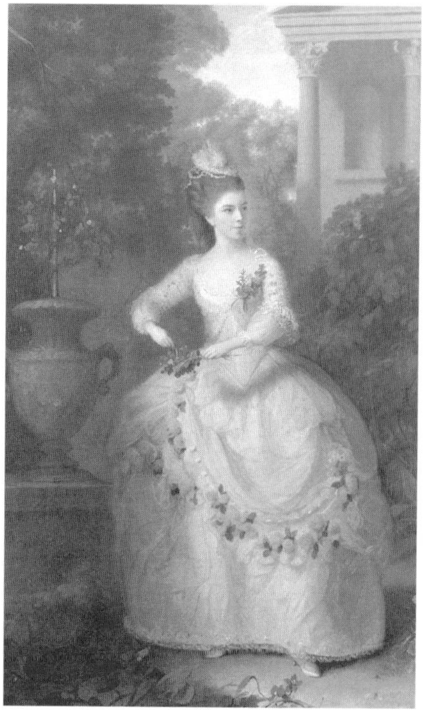

No.25 Thomas Hickey
Frances Abington as Lady Bab in 'The Maid of the Oaks' by John Burgoyne, 1775
Oil on canvas, 88.3 x 52.1 cm
The Garrick Club

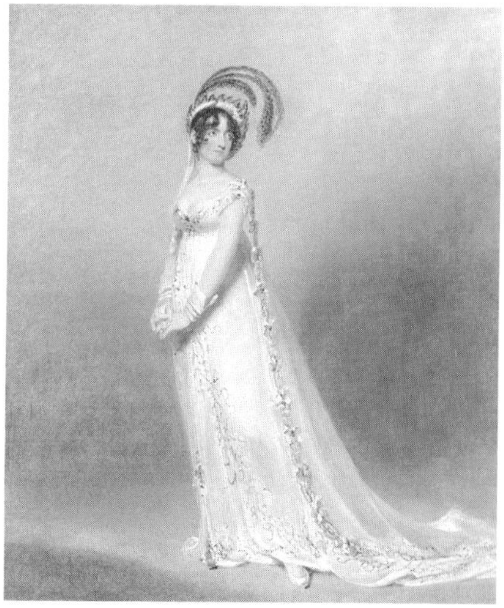

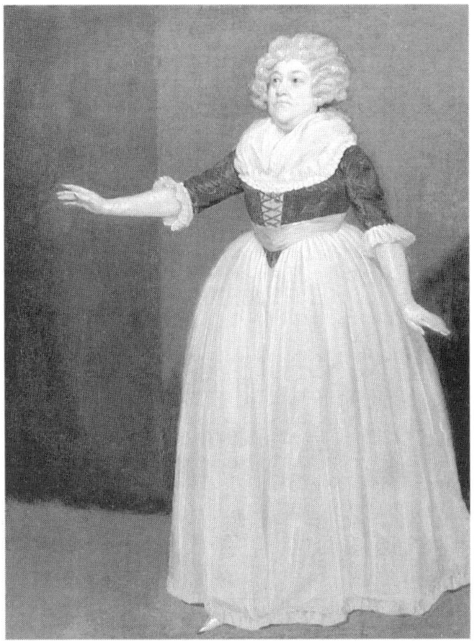

No.27 Samuel De Wilde
Mrs Webb as Lady Dove in 'The Brothers' by Richard Cumberland, c.1792
Oil on canvas, 37.2 x 28.5 cm
The Garrick Club

the point: she is too dazzling for her own good. *The Honey Moon* is an entirely typical moral fable illustrating the Rousseauian principle that no woman can be really loveable unless she has done time in a cottage. Juliana here prepares to marry a Duke: 'Do I to the life', she asks (ominously as it turns out), 'appear a Duchess'. As this observation suggests, she isn't really humble enough. So her husband pretends to be a sham Duke and takes her off to honeymoon in a hovel, where they embark upon the usual round of country walks and village dances. Gradually she gets to like it and in this way becomes 'a gentle wife', the 'sterling comfort of a man's life'. At this point it is safe for him to become a Duke again.

This image is a 'before'; the 'after' occurs later in Act IV when she goes to her Village Dance dressed in a 'neat peasant's dress' of white:

> With no more diamonds than those eyes are made of,
> No deeper rubies than compose thy lips,
> Nor pearls more precious than inhabit them.

We are back to the ideal of Ramsay's *Gentle Shepherd* (No.24) and those many fashionable portraits at this date showing noblewomen in just such 'peasant's dress'. With this later description in mind, one sees how Singleton has stressed the sparkle of jewels (as opposed to eyes, lips and teeth) and the artificiality of an attitude self-consciously struck. Even the setting, especially in contrast to Hickey's Mrs Abington, suggests the hearthlessness of a fashion plate.

Juliana and Lady Bab are at least redeemable; the next three women have vices which can only be contained, not eradicated. Again they are stock types. Lady Dove (No.27) is a termagant; she henpecks her cowardly husband, Sir Benjamin Dove, until a duel on her behalf unexpectedly teaches him courage. From then on he is 'unalterably resolv'd ... to be sole and absolute in this house, master of my own servants, father to my own child, and sovereign lord and governour, Madam, over my own wife'. That counts as a happy ending. Lady Dove is here shown banishing one of her husband's oldest friends in a posture of unfeminine imperiousness.

Opposite:
No.26 Henry Singleton
Maria Davison as Juliana in 'The Honey Moon' by John Tobin
Exhibited at the RA 1805
Oil on canvas, 76.5 x 63.5 cm
The Garrick Club

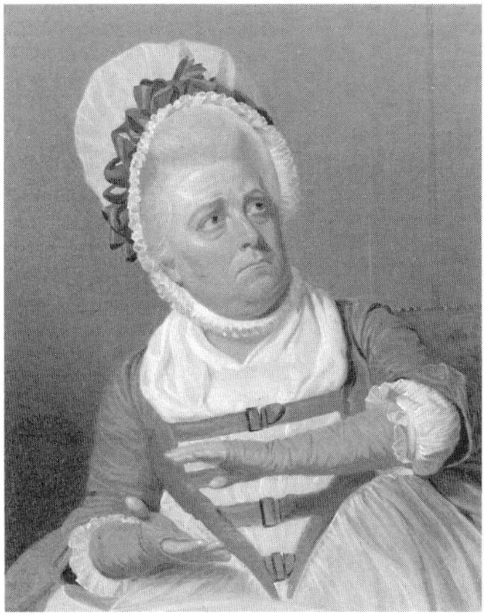

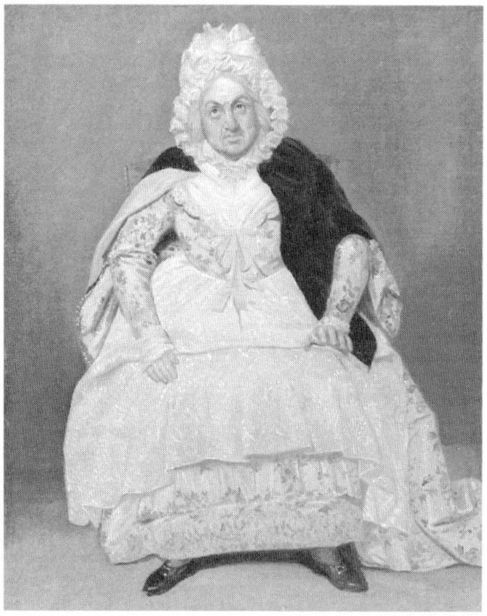

Far left:
No.28 Samuel De Wilde
Mary Ann Davenport as Mrs Moral in 'The Birth-Day' by Thomas Dibdin, c.1805
Oil on panel, 24.5 x 20 cm
The Garrick Club

Left:
No.29 Samuel De Wilde
Henry Angelo as Mrs Cole in 'The Minor' by Samuel Foote
Oil on canvas, 36.5 x 28 cm
The Garrick Club

Mrs Moral (No.28) is a prude. This type (a variant of the old maid) is generally characterised by humble birth, social aspiration, advancing years, avarice, hypocrisy and an instinctive antipathy towards good humour, forgiveness and natural affection. Mrs Moral is housekeeper to the good Captain Bertram; she is here shown refusing to drink his health on his birthday because drinking is 'both immoral and ungenteel'. Typical! De Wilde shows the very image of a canting sour-faced, overdressed hypocrite.

It is clear from this degenerating sequence of women that each looks more masculine than the last. Mrs Cole (No.29) is so bad that she has to be played by a man. This was one of Bannister's favourite parts, but here we see Henry Angelo, who made his one and only appearance on the London stage in this part, at Bannister's request for his benefit, on 29 May 1792.[82]

Mrs Cole is a pious procuress. Needless to say her piety is not of the wholesome, rational, Church of England variety: after flirting with Catholicism, she has fallen under the spell of some accommodating Methodists. 'There had I been', she recalls, 'tossing in a sea of sin, without rudder or compass. And had not the good gentleman [Mr Squintum, her total-immersion guru] piloted me into the harbour of grace, I must have ... been quite swallowed up in the whirlpool of despair. He was the precious instrument of my spiritual sprinkling. –

But however, Sir George, if your mind be set upon a young country thing, to-morrow night, I declare, I can furnish you'. The same Sir George remarks 'with what ease she reconciles her new birth to her old calling!' Henry Angelo enacts the reconciliation: a lumpy, gouty body and a twisted, brutal man's face, and yet his eyes roll up to heaven in an expression of gin-soaked beatitude.

Charles Mathews

Charles Mathews (1776–1835) was one of the most successful comedians of the Regency age. His appearance was against him: he was so thin that he was known as 'stick' to his friends, one of whom (William Lewis) described him as 'the tallest man in the world, and the funniest. He has no regular mouth, but speaks from a little hole in his cheek'.[83] Turning these disadvantages to good comic effect, Mathews took over from John Emery as principal 'low comedian' at York Theatre, and moved to London in 1803 in order to follow in the footsteps of another comic bean-pole, Richard Suett (see No.20).[84] Mathews used his considerable earnings in order to amass the best private collection of theatrical paintings in history. These pictures formed the core of the Garrick Club Collection and all but seven of the works in this exhibition.

Mathews started collecting as early as 1803; he took advantage of previous collectors' sales (such as that of the Covent Garden Manager, Harris, in 1819 when he acquired over 40 works including our Nos.9 and 10); he also commissioned works himself (including Nos.6 and 40). His hoard of nearly 400 works was displayed in a Gallery specially built in 1819 at his Gothic retreat, Ivy Cottage. The packed hanging style at Ivy Cottage – frame to frame, floor to ceiling – was remarkably similar to that of Dulwich Picture Gallery, which had opened to the public only two years earlier. The subsequent history of Mathews's pictures will also sound familiar to visitors of this Gallery. He tried unsuccessfully to interest the recently-founded National Gallery in this unique record of the British stage. In 1833 he exhibited 388 items at the Queen's Bazaar, but the takings were modest and no buyer came forward. Finally in 1835 he sold the lot to the Garrick Club for £1,000, a third of his original asking price.

Mathews sought records of past and living actors not only from a passion for the theatre, but also because they fuelled his own performances. From the very beginning of his career Mathews made his name as a mimic, on and off stage. While playing familiar parts – like the down-at-heal actor, Tag, in *The Spoiled Child* (see No.21, p.33) – he introduced imitations of real actors to great applause.[85] He also developed the habit of observing ordinary people in order to mimic them. He could disguise himself so as to be mistaken for another for the entire duration of a dinner party; he could render and switch characters with 'a versatility that knew no bounds, a felicity which afforded unceasing delight, and a fidelity which did not admit of an improvement'.[86] These talents were all on display in Mathews's one-man shows, which were so successful that he gave up all other conventional acting for the last decades of his career. The playbill for the first of these shows, given on 12 April 1808, gives some idea of their character: 'Mr Mathews (with the occasional assistance of Mrs Mathews in the vocal department) will exhibit an entire "New Entertainment", consisting of recitations, songs, imitations, ventriloquy, &c, entitled "The Mail Coach; or Rambles in Yorkshire" ... [this includes] imitation of an Idiot catching a fly ... imitation of "Fond Barney"' and 'Imitations of some of the principal London performers'.[87]

Two of the characters mentioned in the 1808 show were still in his repertoire for a performance in 1813 in front of Queen Charlotte, which was said to be the one immortalised in Harlow's painting of Mathews in five different characters (No.30). On the far left is 'Fond Barney', one of the many simpletons who, according to Anne Mathews, were particularly well-liked and cared for in York.[88] He sold racing calendars and 'last dying speeches' at York Racecourse and regularly muddled the two. The figure in the centre is also 'a study from another of these harmless beings' who spent the day catching flies.[89] The figures second and third from the left come from plays: the fat Mr Wiggins from Allingham's *The Birthday* and Buskin, a poor actor, from Theodore Edward Hook's *Killing no Murder*. Buskin is in a way the summary of the whole painting as the part

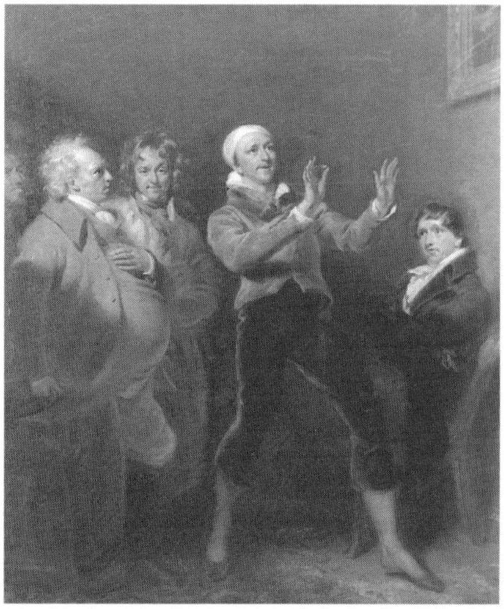

No.30 George Henry Harlow
Charles Mathews as Fond Barney; as Mr Wiggins in 'Mistress Wiggins'; as Buskin in 'Killing no Murder'; as an idiot catching flies; and as himself
Oil on canvas, 74.3 x 61.6 cm
The Garrick Club

requires multiple mimicry. At one point he offers to impersonate a whole retinue of servants in order to pay his board at an inn. An imperious Nabob is then served in rapid succession by a boot-catcher, French hair-dresser, cook and waiter; the only complication occurring when he demands two services at once. Harlow's portrait shows Mathews's face as Buskin staring straight out with a comical, asymmetrical and mobile character as if caught in the act of melting from one character into another. It provides a way into the extraordinary contrasts in the faces one either side: the coarse Barney balancing the worldly image of Mathews as himself; the determined Mr Wiggins contrasting with the vacant idiot.

The 1817 engraving of this painting carries an explanation saying that 'the characters introduced are all taken from life', including 'an extraordinary fat man whose manners and appearance suggested the idea of Mr Wiggins'.[90] This serves to remind us that Mathews was a comedian in a modern sense: one who would have considerable say

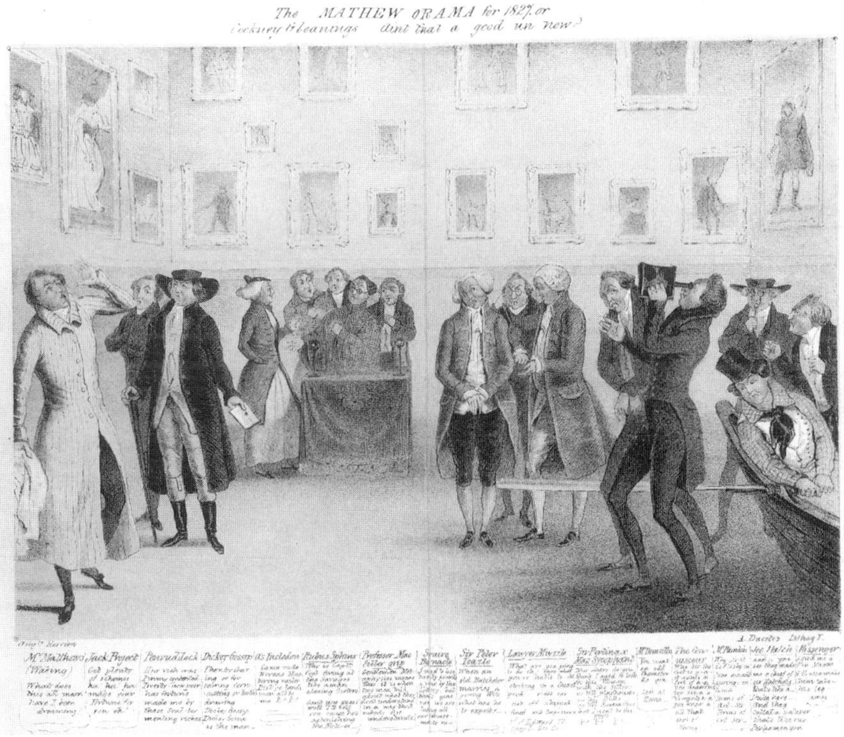

Fig.13 A *Matheworama* or one-man show, illustrated in Anne Mathews, *Memoirs of Charles Mathews*, 1838 The London Library

in his own 'material', even if actually written by another. According to Anne Mathews, all the parts her husband created 'at least for many years, were in fact mere outlines left for him to fill up by dint of his genius, by authors who felt it necessary to write *words* for others. One of his most popular characters, Buskin, in *Killing no Murder*, was almost all his own, except the situations'.[91] The note also goes on to explain Mathews's presence *in propria persona:* "The intention of the artist is to present a portrait of Mr Mathews as STUDYING those characters for imitation preserving at the same time his likeness as varied in the representation of each'.[92] This explains the look of quizzical astonishment on Mathews's own 'confounded crooked face' (as he called it): it is as if he cannot bring himself to believe the eccentricities of fellow humans or else his own powers of imitation.[93]

It is this idea of imitation – of an actor studying nature in order to invent characters – which brings acting up to the level of writing and likens it to painting. Mathews played on this analogy between a mimed and a painted portrait. Some of his monopolylogues (as they were called) took place against a set displaying his collection of acting portraits (see Fig.13). During one, the portraits seemed to come to life as he mimicked the performances of Suett, Kemble, Cooke and King. He developed a theory of mimicry as a means of theatrical immortalisation, as something which could take over the role traditionally ascribed to painting. A description of one of his *At Homes* explains this game of generational Chinese whispers: 'His Gallery, he says, he has collected for the purpose of catching inspiration from the mimic semblances of the mighty masters of the art, an art declared by Colley Cibber and Garrick, whose words he quotes, to perish with the artist; this Mr. Mathews denies, he says, imitation, which has grown into disrepute of late days ... can perpetuate both the art and the artist ... I knew Tate Wilkinson, he knew Garrick; Garrick knew Betterton; Betterton knew Booth; Booth knew Davenant, who was Shakespeare's godson; Davenant knew Ben Jonson, and Ben Jonson was Shakespeare's friend. Now had they possessed the power of handing down imitation from each other, I might this evening put Shakespeare before you'.[94]

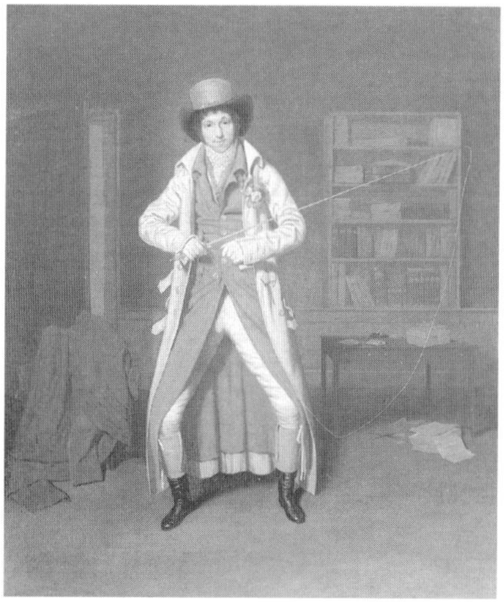

No.31 Samuel De Wilde
Charles Mathews as Dick Cypher in 'Hit or Miss' by Isaac Pocock, 1810
Oil on canvas, 75.5 x 63.5 cm
The Garrick Club

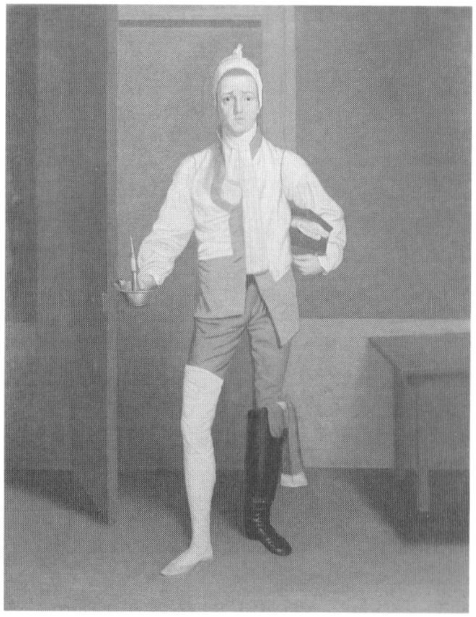

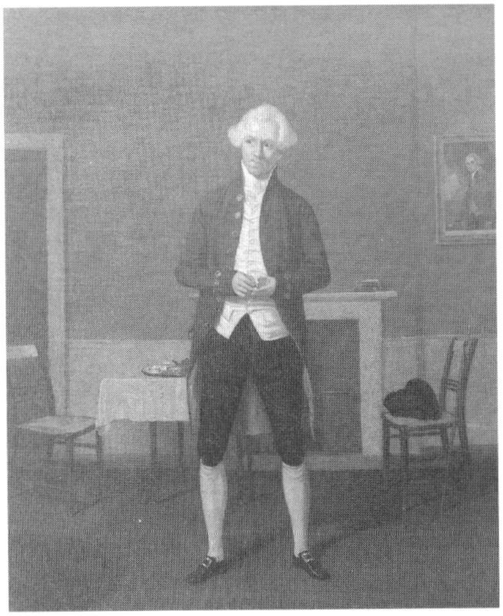

No.33 Samuel De Wilde
Charles Mathews as Sir Fretful Plagiary in 'The Critic' by Richard Brinsley Sheridan, 1810
Oil on canvas, 73.7 x 57.2 cm
The Garrick Club

Opposite:
No.32 Samuel De Wilde
Charles Mathews as Somno in 'The Sleepwalker or Which is the Lady?' by Wally Chamberlain Oulton
Oil on canvas, 77 x 58.3 cm
The Garrick Club

These two images of Mathews by his friend Samuel De Wilde (Nos.31 and 32) depict him as characters which the authors were happy to acknowledge were in part the actor's creation.[95] Dick Cypher is a typical member of the then-fashionable 'Bang up Club'. This was a group of men of fortune who bought and drove their own stage-coaches. Their paid coach-men sat idly by and yet the club members themselves dressed rather like dandified coach-men. Dick Cypher's outfit can be recognised from Anne Mathews's description: 'the costume of each gentleman consisted of a bottle-green body-coat, a milk-white double-breasted great coat, reaching to the heels, several large capes, and buttons of mother-of-pearl, as large as crown pieces; a many-flowered *bouquet* in a button-hole at the side; upon the head a low-crowned broad-brimmed hat, with a broad riband and buckle, the hair sleeked under it coachman like'.[96] In Pocock's farce Cypher is a member of the 'Neck or Nothing' club, an urban bumpkin and Regency boy-racer, so horsy and slangy of speech that everyone takes him for a servant. Here he sings his song in praise of horse-power (at the end of Act II), in a giddy-up posture as if charging the audience.

The visual comedy of both these images depends upon the central, frontal and symmetrical presentation of the figure, a toy-soldier effect increased by Mathews's 'Maypole' physique. Cypher is a chirpy gentleman; Somno a tragic servant. Another 'resting' actor making ends meet, Somno sleep-walks uttering disconnected fragments from his store of tragic Shakespearean parts. His entry recalls Lady Macbeth, who (until Mrs Siddons) always carried a candle in her sleep-walking scene: 'Enter Somno ... asleep ludicrously dressed, in his night-cap; a candlestick in one hand, and a dressing box in the other. After looking around wildly, he approaches the table'. He blurts Shakespeare at his most sublime, though some wires get crossed: 'who would have thought the old man to have had so much blood in him?' becomes 'Damme, didn't think I had so much pluck in me'. This scene is a travesty of sublimity, a mock-heroic. We recognise the visual devices: the rugger-ball face marked out with the diagrammatic lines of Le Brunian horror; the towering rigidity of John Philip Kemble at his most imperious. It is probable that in this part (as in others) Mathews guyed Kemble's famously imitable style. All these things are deflated by the ludicrous asymmetry of the costume, which makes an kind of impromptu motley (compare No.14).

Supposedly a portrait of Richard Cumberland, Sir Fretful (No.33) is a playwright of thin talent and thinner skin, who affects to despise the admiration he craves. We see him, with a grim determination and mounting fury, laughing off some bad reviews. Leigh Hunt 'never yet saw so perfect a representation of rage, and pretended enjoyment' as Mathews exhibited in this part, his laughing 'like a tickled man with the tooth-ache'.[97] De Wilde clearly shows the mouth curled upwards, stiffening into a 'most dreary smile' (as Hunt put it), while his frowning glare shows his true feelings. Everything about the posture – the sway of the body, the suspicious turn of the head, the fumbling for snuff – suggests fretful irresolution.

In the last of these pictures Mathews is shown in another 'real-life' incident, which he had observed in Boston (No.34). Every day, Monsieur Mallet, a French émigré, inquired at the post-restante for a letter from his daughter; every day he was told that there was none and was left wondering how she could have forgotten 'her poor old father'. Of course the letter was there all along, only the functionary was looking under 'Malley' not 'Mallet'.[98] It was in this part that Mathews 'established his power for the pathetic'.[99] In this image he appears as both Mallet and the postman in order to provide a contrast between the sad and stoical dignity of the European aristocracy and the ill-mannered stupidity of the Republican lower orders (which Mathews himself frequently remarked upon).

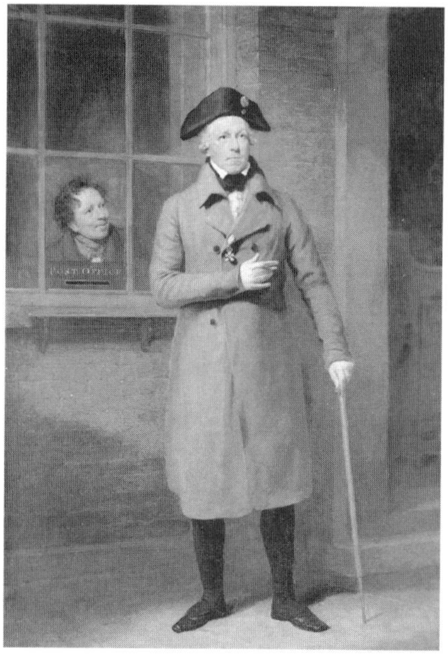

No.34 George Clint
Charles Mathews as Monsieur Mallet in 'Monsieur Mallet or My Daughter's Letter' by William Thomas Moncrieff
Oil on canvas, 82.5 x 56 cm
The Garrick Club

Acting and Painting

The title of this exhibition refers to the art of theatrical painting as well as that of acting. When considering this special branch of painting it is important to remember that it is an amalgam of two forms and yet is distinct from both. Its nearest ancestor, especially in comedy, is genre, or the depiction of everyday life. The Dutch masters of the seventeenth century excelled in this department and taught English followers, like Hogarth, the importance of a faithful, atmospheric and expressive depiction of interiors. Charles Lamb said of Hogarth that he could tell a story in furniture. This is all the more important for theatrical painting as, unlike even Hogarth's brand of genre, it illustrates a specific text.

In their rhetorical expression the works in this exhibition might be taken for history paintings (that is depictions of literary stories); Lawrence even called a theatrical portrait (like Nos.5 and 6) 'a sort of half-history picture'.[100] Yet theatrical painting is different in that it depicts a particular individual playing a timeless hero – delivering the full drama of the situation and yet allowing us to imagine that the actor could step out of character if he so wished. This requires a kind of distance, a self-conscious exaggeration, which allows the gesture or expression to draw attention to itself, perhaps even (though this is a risky adventure in tragedy) to point up some contrast between the actor and the part. Such a distance is all the more important for comedy.

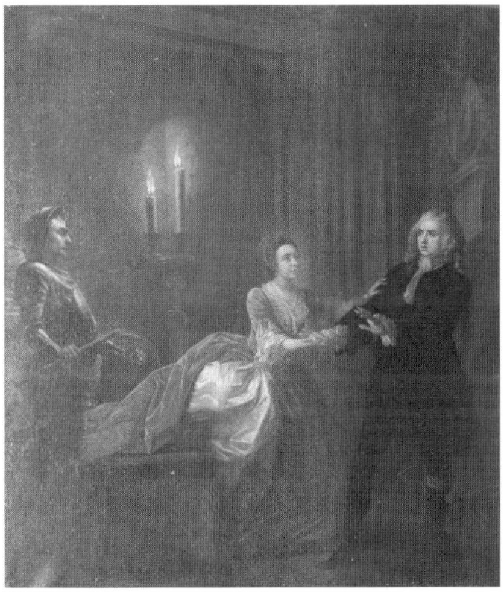

No.35 Francis Hayman
Spranger Barry as Hamlet, Mary Elmy as Gertrude and Lacy Ryan as the Ghost in 'Hamlet'
Oil on canvas, 127 x 108 cm
The Garrick Club

The art of theatrical painting depends upon juggling these different traditions and levels of reality in order to create a pictorial equivalent (rather than mere record) of the stage spectacle. Hayman's *Hamlet* (No.35) inclines towards history. The artist worked freely in all types of painting – history, genre, portraiture, and scene-painting – and is clearly seeking to reconcile his ideal image of this moment of the play with a specific performance. The scenery is imaginary; the candle-light dramatic, but impossible in a theatre of this date.[101] The strange ring of blue light surrounding the flame is a paranormal phenomenon, derived from Shakespearean belief that lights burn blue

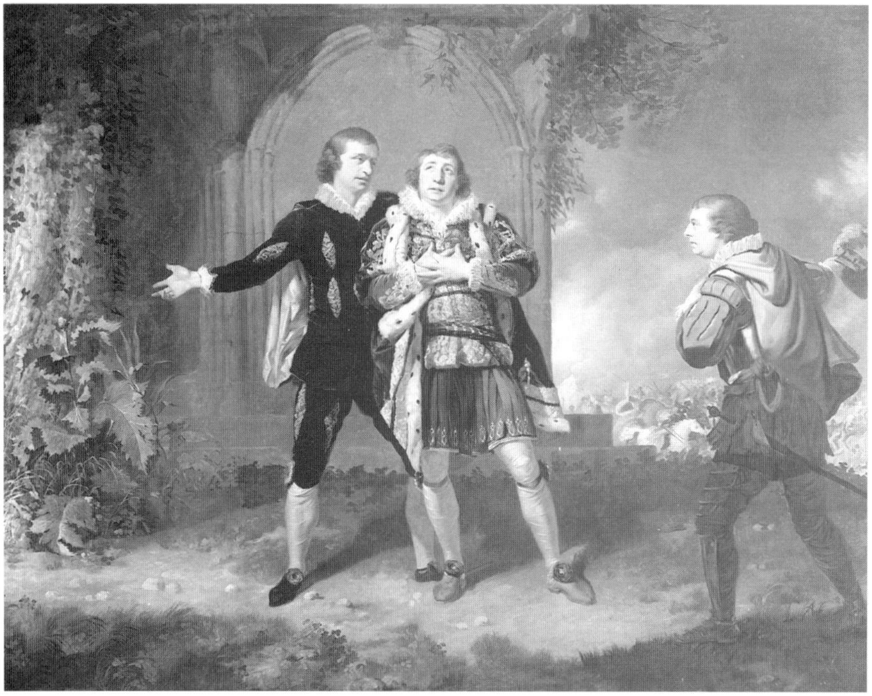

No.36 John Hamilton Mortimer
Robert Bensley as Hubert, William Powell as King John and R. Smith as a Messenger in 'King John'
Oil on canvas, 101 x 127 cm
The Garrick Club

in the presence of ghosts (see *Richard III*, Act V, scene 3, l.181). The lighting on the figures is manipulated so that the living receive a much stronger glare than the pallid moonlight which bleaches out the colour from the face and armour of the ghost. The background here also plays tricks on the eye: partly suggestive of a mirror, partly of an aperture, we seem to be looking at a material through which only a ghost might pass. It is perhaps even deliberate that Gertrude starts up from her chair to help Hamlet (she doesn't see the ghost), and in this way leaves an empty throne to her right hand which her husband should be occupying.

All these are stage-directions and 'special effects' supplied by the artist; the performances are stately rather than electric, in the 'Pre-Garrick' manner. 'Silver-tongued' Barry (1719–77), as he was called, was apparently 'full of grace and dignity', but 'was deficient in representing the violent emotions of the soul; nor could a countenance so placid as his ever wear the strong impressions of despair or horror'.[102]

The popularity of *King John* in the eighteenth century is something of a mystery (No.36). It is probable that its splendidly villainous

Cardinal Pandulph and explicity anti-papal message made it a favourite amongst the John Bulls in the audience, obssessed with the threat of Catholic France. It is clear from the costumes that its historical character is more important than *Hamlet*'s (Hayman's painting being only a decade earlier). It was the same play which announced the fully authentic series of history plays produced by Charles Kemble in collaboration with the playwright and antiquarian James Robinson Planché in 1827.

The moment shown in Mortimer's painting is Act V, scene 3, when a messenger announces an English victory over the French in the battle raging in the background. King John, having been poisoned by a monk ('a resolved villain'), is supported by his faithful ally, Hubert, who will bear him away to Swinstead Abbey to die. This Abbey is suggested by the Gothic ruin behind the King, which also provides a frame for him as he expires with all the trappings of sanctity – eyes turned up, face catching the light and hands pressed to the heart. The King is a martyr dying at the moment of victory. Such a patriotic image would strike a chord in the audience at this time, as recollections of General Wolfe's death defending Quebec were still fresh and the episode was celebrated in Edward Penny's painting recently exhibited at the Society of Artists in 1764.

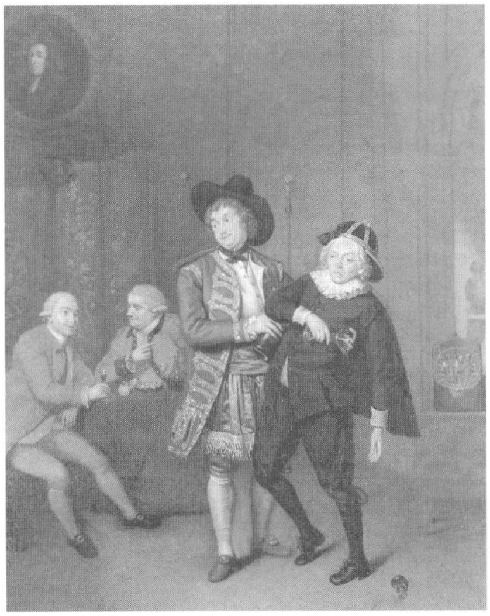

No.37 Benjamin Vandergucht
John Moody as Teague, William Parsons as Obadiah, Thomas Jefferson as Colonel Restless and James Aickin as Colonel Blunt in 'The Committee' by Sir Robert Howard
Oil on canvas, 126.5 x 100.5 cm
The Garrick Club

Vandergucht's painting (No.37) is probably the most self-explanatory work in the exhibition. The play deals with the Commonwealth period, when the Committee of the title was busy confiscating the estates of Royalists. It remained popular throughout the eighteenth century, allowing audiences a horrified glimpse of the combined evils of Puritanism, hypocrisy, disloyalty to the monarch and denial of the sacred rights of property. At this moment Teague, the loyal and resourceful Irish servant of the two threatened Cavaliers drinking behind, brings on Obadiah, the secretary of the Committee, having got him blind drunk. Teague and Obadiah make a now familiar contrast between noble and plebeian posture (Teague is clearly awarded honorary nobility) and between cheerful, indulgent good-humour and sour-faced Puritanism. Though Obadiah has drunk, we actually see him emptying his glass and throwing his snuff to the ground, as if instinctively repudiating the wicked stuff.

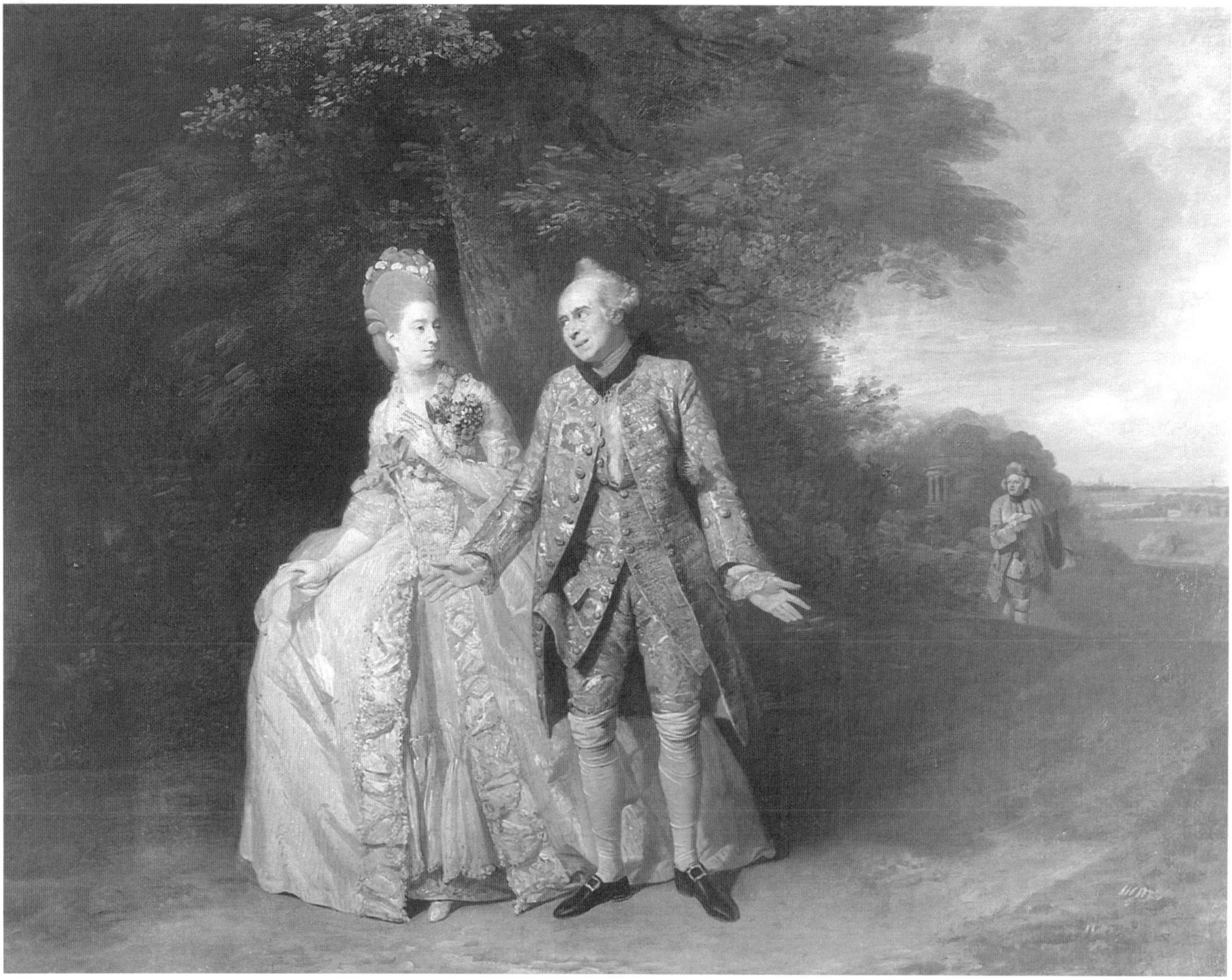

In the most brilliantly comic painting in the Garrick collection (No.38), Zoffany effortlessly sails a course between depicting a real and a stage event. The trees are just bland enough to be stage-flats and just leafy enough to be trees; the brightly picked-out figures have just a hint of stiffness and isolation from the simple background to suggest the glitter of costume in the footlights. The gestures and expressions have just enough of exaggeration to freeze a moment of comic posturing, and celebrate a great actor's ability to be larger than life.

No.38 Johan Zoffany
Sophia Baddeley as Fanny Sterling, Robert Baddeley as Canton and Thomas King as Lord Ogleby in 'The Clandestine Marriage' by David Garrick and George Colman the Elder
Oil on canvas, 102 x 128 cm
The Garrick Club

Old King with every requisite to please,
Strong sense, dry humour, wit, and comic ease,
Unrivall'd reigns on Drury's classic boards,
In crusty crabbed sires, and testy lords.[103]

This is Thomas King's mention in *The Druriad;* the most famous of all testy Lords in King's repertoire was Lord Ogleby, a part he created. Ogleby is a burnt-out gallant, kept alive by a daily administering of nostrums and potions, who is nonetheless 'full of attentions to the ladies, and smiles, and grins, and leers, and ogles, and fills every wrinkle in his old wizen face with comical expressions of tenderness' (Act I, scene 1). Ogleby is really only testy on account of his ailments; deep down he has a heart of gold. The moment depicted here is the one of maximum comic entanglement. Ogleby is staying with Sterling, a rich merchant, to negotiate an advantageous marriage between his impoverished nephew and Sterling's daughter, Fanny. Unfortunately Fanny is already secretly married and chooses this moment to come clean. However her manner of presenting the case is so modestly round-about, so full of unspecific references to secret passion, that Ogleby thinks she is declaring her love for him. Of course he can't resist.

Ogleby: There's no standing this: I have caught the infection – her tenderness dissolves me. *(sighs)*

Fanny: And should you too severly judge of a rash action which passion prompted, and modesty has long concealed –

Ogleby: *(taking her hand)* Thou amiable creature – command my heart, for it is vanquished. – Speak but thy virtuous wishes and enjoy them.

Fanny: I cannot, my lord ... *(exit in tears)* (Act IV, scene 1).

The comedy of Zoffany's image depends upon the ludicrously unheroic manner of Ogleby's declaration of love. He shrugs his shoulders and smiles a wan, hesitant and apologetic smile. It is as if an instinct of gallantry has talked him into the declaration against his better judgement, as if he is in the grip of a Pavlovian habit of courtship. The nearest precedent for this expression occurs in Reynolds's *Garrick Between Comedy and Tragedy*, where Garrick is shown shrugging his apologies to Tragedy for yielding to his baser comic instincts. Ogleby is also poised in the centre of the painting making a choice – between Fanny or loneliness. It is with visible reluctance that he has decided to put himself under starter's orders for one last time.

George Clint (1770–1854) is nobody's idea of a household name. He made a respectable career out of theatrical painting in his lifetime, though resented never becoming a full Royal Academician. The only indication of any real appreciation of his worth occurs in the price list of Charles Mathews's collection, which sets the highest value of £100 on his scene from *Lock and Key* (No.39) along with Lawrence's *Kemble as Cato* (No.6). Clint came to the fore at a time when stage wings were being replaced by the full 'box sets' of the Victorian era, which recreated the three walls and ceiling of a room, with lavish and believable furnishings and practicable doors. Plays now took place in rooms rather than in front of scenes. These rooms could give a feel for the action, they could characterise their owners as vividly as their costume. Old Brummagen in *Lock and Key* is a stock figure in more ways than one. For the purposes of the action he is the classic Don Basilio – an old botherum of a guardian with a pretty ward. He is also a parvenu obsessed with pedigree, with clothes and a house full of curiosities telling bogus tales of the exploits of his non-existent ancestors. His Spanish dress was supposedly presented to his great uncle by the Queen in a bull-fight; his whole house, according to his servant, 'is like the fine speeches of fine gentry, all counterfeit, and the furniture in it would serve for the scenery of a harlequin farce: it tumbles to pieces the moment it is touched' (Act I, scene 2). The extraordinary richness of surface in Clint's painting – the play of light over silk, brocade, fine porcelain, powdered wigs and carved wood – is a conscious tribute to the great Dutch masters of the seventeenth century, a life-size version of Gabriel Metsu. It is also an index of old Brummagen's gullible vanity.

Cheerly, the juvenile lead, plans to abduct Laura (seen here locked up behind the grille at the back) by means of Brummagen's

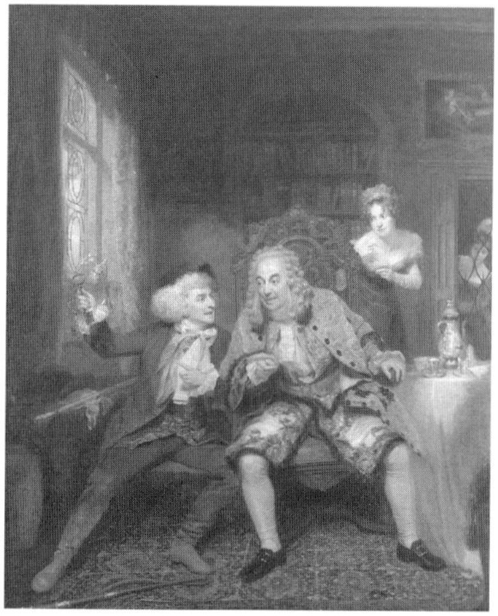

No.39 George Clint
Joseph Munden as Old Brummagem, Marie Cubbitt as Laura, Edward Knight as Ralph and Mary Orger as Fanny in 'Lock and Key' by Prince Hoare
Oil on canvas, 128 x 101.5 cm
The Garrick Club

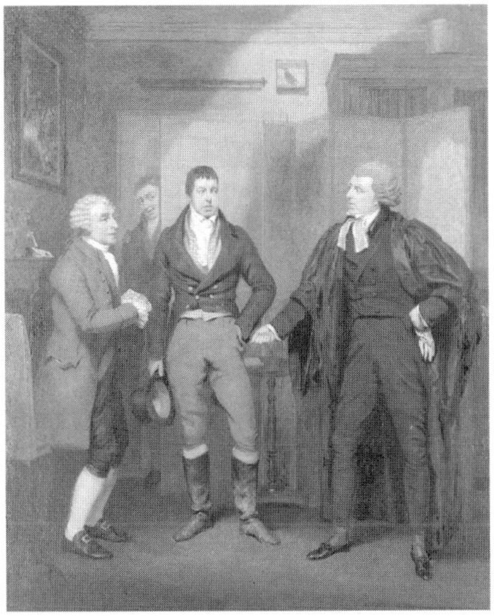

No.40 George Clint
Charles Mathews as Flexible, William Blanchard as Dr Camphor, John Emery as Andrew and John Liston as Lubin Log in 'Love, Law, and Physic' by James Kenney
Oil on canvas, 127 x 101.5 cm
The Garrick Club

servant Ralph, who disguises himself as the steward of a visiting and eligible grandee. Ralph is seen here, dressed to the nines, telling Brummagen about a guardian he knew whose keys were stolen and slipped to a servant. Brummagen listens agog as the very thing he fears happens before his eyes (Act II, scene 4).

This rather obvious comic situation must have been enlivened by the performance as Brummagen of Joseph Munden (1758–1832, see also No.15). Though the two depictions of Munden here seem similar enough, he was renowned at the time for versatility: according to Lamb 'there is one face of Farley, one face of Knight, one (but what a one it is) of Liston; but Munden has none that you can properly pin down and call his'; in short he was 'not a comedian but a company'.

John Liston (1776–1846), a 'cockney' comic mentioned above who specialised in low comedy, is shown here (No.40) in one of his favourite parts – the boorishly rich timber-merchant, Lubin Log (standing in the centre). Clint's painting was commissioned by Charles Mathews and may have been intended to bring together as many of the reigning comedians of the day as possible. Mathews himself plays Flexible (to the right), a plausible, good-humoured and unscrupulous lawyer helping his friend to get the girl. Log is the rival suitor and Dr Camphor (to the left), a local apothecary, is the uncle and guardian. In this part William Blanchard (1769–1835) displays his powers in the rendering of 'vocal countrymen': his genteel costume and wig cannot conceal the rusticity of his parallel-footed, bent-kneed posture.[104] At this moment Flexible is maintaining spuriously that his friend Danvers is the true heir to the Log fortune. 'Do you mean you can prove black is white?', asks the bewildered Log. 'Sir', replies Flexible, 'black is white; shall a timber-merchant dare contest me in points of law?'.

According to Leigh Hunt, Charles Kemble, John Philip's younger brother, excelled in tender lovers, tragic gentlemen and 'very happy mixture of the occasional debauchee and gentleman of feeling'.[105] The perfect example of the last category is Charles II in Payne's play *The Merry Monarch* of 1824 (No.41). He is seen here on an incognito jaunt to a pub called the Great Admiral with the Earl of Rochester, who leaves him with no money to pay the bill. When he offers his watch as payment, the honest innkeeper, Captain Copp, demands 'How came you by this watch?', naturally assuming that he has stolen it.

We again see a familiar contrast between Copp's downright bluff vehemence and Charles's natural elegance and authority of posture, which no down-dressing can conceal. But the meaning is subtly different, for here both low and high life are celebrated. Charles and Rochester are in the tavern to 'study human nature in all its varieties' and particularly to learn to value rough diamonds like Copp. This is part of the British myth of the democratic monarch: a courtier later refers to Charles as 'accessible to the people'; Copp when he finally recognises him addresses him as 'Mr King'. The history of the early years of the nineteenth century must have given this image a reassuring patriotic resonance. If this is what British monarchs are really like how secure they can feel. A king who can deal with plain-speaking subjects so cheerfully need fear no revolution, on the recent French model. Charles, it implies, was restored by the love of the people, not by a victorious foreign army as in post-Napoleonic France. More specifically this image might express the vain hope that the debauched and hated George IV might somehow turn out to be a loveable old rogue in the manner of Charles II.

The room tells more of the story here than in any previous example. Its simple tiles and whitewashed walls convey a sturdy homeliness and virtue, while its exotic touches – map, painting, Chinese screen, porcelain punch bowl, glasses, caps and smoking jackets – convey the increasing wealth and expanding trade of the Restoration period. We see a great seafaring power in its infancy. Even the consciously Rembrandtesque character of the painting – the plastery texture of the wall and floor, and the soft misty light – reinforce a sense of Britain taking over from Holland as the world's naval power. Charles stands four-square in front of a map, as if he carries the world on his sturdy shoulders. He jocularly remarks of their night's escapade that 'His lordship left the whole weight of – business – upon my shoulders'. Obviously a celebration of naval power has an especially meaning after Trafalgar, when the name Great Admiral

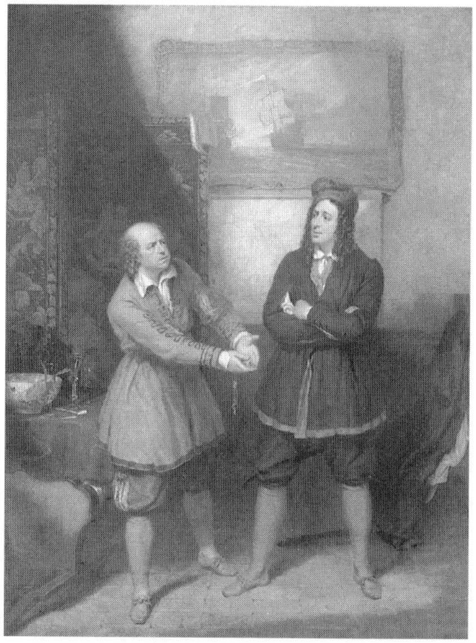

No.41 George Clint
John Fawcett as Captain Copp and Charles Kemble as the King in 'Charles the Second or the Merry Monarch' by John Howard Payne
Oil on canvas, 115 x 85 cm
The Garrick Club

instantly called to mind not Blake or some veteran of the Anglo-Dutch wars but Horatio Nelson.

The most prolific theatrical artist, and the most represented in this exhibition, is Samuel De Wilde (1748–1832). Son of a Dutch immigrant woodcarver, he was a master of the Dutch speciality of small-scale finely-detailed painting. He was type-cast as a theatrical specialist after his series of images of actors in role produced for the 1791–7 editions of Bell's popular collections of plays, *British Theatre*. His great gift is tactical artificiality. Mathews as Somno (No.32) is convincing in the sense that it is legible, but it doesn't actually look like a man in a room. The furniture is far too simple, the composition too contrived, the pose too regular, the expression too diagrammatic; even the paint surface has the glossy polish of a wax-work, rather than flesh and blood. In part this is a faithful record of the special reality of the stage: of wobbly sets, over-acting, grease-paint and footlights. In part it is a deliberately invented pictorial equivalent of this stage-reality: a kind of tongue-in-cheek hamming it up in paint.

Notes

1 Mrs Anne Mathews, *Memoirs of Charles Mathews*, 4 vols., London 1838, II, pp.283–4.
2 Letter from Dr Hoadly to Garrick, 23 May 1765, quoted in David Thomas and Arnold Hare, *Restoration and Georgian England, 1660–1788*, Cambridge 1989, p.255.
3 *Catalogue of Pictures in Possession of the Garrick Club*, London 1909, p.55, no.120, and Geoffrey Ashton (edited by Kalman A. Burnim and Andrew Wilton), *Pictures in the Garrick Club*, 1997, no.726.
4 See the 1709 Rowe edition of Shakespeare (Simon Trussler, *The Cambridge Illustrated History of the British Theatre*, Cambridge 1994, p.132).
5 Jane Williamson, *Charles Kemble, Man of the Theatre*, Univeristy of Nebraska 1970, p.3 quotes Westland Marston, *Our Recent Actors*, Boston 1888, pp.113–14.
6 John Hill, *The Actor*, 1755, p.239, quoted in Thomas and Hare 1989, p.345.
7 Trussler 1994, pp.174–5.
8 Kalman A. Burnim, *David Garrick Director*, University of Pittsburgh 1961, p.107.
9 *The Gentleman's Magazine*, 1742, quoted in The Arts Council, *The Georgian Playhouse*, 1975; see also Cecil Price, *Theatre in the Age of Garrick*, Oxford 1973, p.25.
10 Burnim 1961, p.59.
11 Thomas and Hare 1989, p.327; Hill 1755.
12 Price 1973, p.20; *Dramatic Miscellanies*, Dublin 1784.
13 Price 1973, p.3.
14 Burnim 1961, p.1.
15 Price 1973, p.18.
16 Theophilus Cibber, quoted in Price 1973, p.15.
17 See Jennifer Montagu, *The Expression of the Passions*, New Haven and London 1994, p.85, and John Adolphus, *Memoirs of John Bannister, Comedian*, London 1839, I, pp.30–1.
18 Charles Macklin, *The Art and Duty of an Actor*, quoted by George Taylor in '"The Just Delineation of the Passions": Theories of Acting in the Age of Garrick' in Kenneth Richards and Peter Thomson (eds.), *The Eighteenth-Century English Stage*, London 1972, p.57.
19 Aaron Hill, *Essay on the Art of Acting*, 1746, quoted in Taylor 1972, pp.64–5.
20 Thomas and Hare 1989, p.45; Roger Pickering, *Reflections upon Theatrical Expression in Tragedy*, 1755, p.31.
21 See The Arts Council 1975, no.29.
22 Thomas and Hare 1989, p.377; *The Theatrical Review*, 1763.
23 Thomas and Hare 1989, pp.317–19.
24 James Boaden, *Memoirs of the Life of John Philip Kemble*, 2 vols., London 1825, p.xiv, quoted in Burnim 1961, pp.66–7.
25 Price 1973, p.68.
26 See *Recollections of the Life of John O'Keeffe*, 1826, quoted in The Arts Council 1975, no.288.
27 See Burnim 1961, p.80.
28 Burnim 1961, p.97.
29 The Arts Council 1975, nos.232–9.
30 Trussler 1994, p.221.
31 Kelly 1980, p.99.
32 Kelly 1980, pp.34–5.
33 Kelly 1980, p.47.
34 George III's opinion, quoted in Kelly 1980, p.22; see also Burnim 1961, pp.55, 60.
35 Trussler 1994, p.207.
36 Kelly 1980, p.202.
37 Kelly 1980, p.181.
38 Kelly 1980, p.87.
39 Kelly 1980, p.22.
40 Thomas and Hare 1989, p.364; Trussler 1994, p.208.
41 Kelly 1980, p.49.
42 James Boaden, *Memoirs of Mrs Siddons*, II, 1827, pp.288–92, quoted in Thomas and Hare 1989, p.49.
43 Kelly 1980, p.69.
44 Mathews 1838, II, p.223.
45 Ashton 1997, no.306.
46 Ashton 1997, no.306.
47 Garrick Catalogue 1909, p.101.
48 Tate Wilkinson's memoirs of 1791, quoted in Thomas and Hare 1989, pp.321–2.
49 Thomas and Hare 1989, pp.330–1.
50 Thomas and Hare 1989, p.329.
51 *St James Chronicle*, 30 October 1773, quoted in Price 1973, p.59.

52 Thomas and Hare 1989, pp.330–1.
53 Kelly 1980, p.102, see also p.74.
54 James Robinson Planché, *Recollections and Reflections*, London 1872, p.36.
55 See Williamson 1970, p.167.
56 Williamson 1970, p.7.
57 Kelly 1980, pp.159–60.
58 Jean Genest, *Some Account of the English Stage*, Bath 1832, VIII, p.194, quoted by A. Hare, in Richards and Thomson (eds.) 1972, pp.131–2.
59 Thomas and Hare 1989, p.374; *The Monthly Mirror*, November 1800, pp.318–21.
60 Quoted by Hare 1972, p.130.
61 Joseph Donohue, *Theatre in the Age of Kean*, Oxford 1975, p.59.
62 Brian Dobbs, *Drury Lane, Three Centuries of the Theatre Royal, 1663–1971*, London 1972.
63 Kelly 1980, p.198.
64 Donohue 1975, p.59.
65 Mathews 1838, II, p.258.
66 Mathews 1838, III, p.156.
67 Mathews 1838, I, p.350 (Colman to Mathews 23 October 1802).
68 Burnim 1961, p.56.
69 See Anthony Pasquin, *The Children of Thespis: A Poem*, London 1786, and Ashton 1997, introduction.
70 See Colman letter to Mathews 23 October 1802, in Mathews 1838, I, p.350.
71 Garrick Catalogue 1909, p.89.
72 Adolphus 1839, I, pp.30–1.
73 *The Letters of the Earl of Chesterfield to his Son*, 2 vols., London 1901, I, p.140 (letter of 29 November 1745).
74 Ashton 1997, no.782.
75 The Arts Council 1975, no.125.
76 Thomas and Hare 1989, p.414.
77 Price 1973, p.197; *A Dissertation on Comedy*, 1750, p.15.
78 Ashton 1997, no.392.
79 Charles Dibdin, *Complete History of the English Stage, 1797–1800*, V, pp.357–9, quoted in Thomas and Hare 1989, pp.388–89.
80 Adolphus 1839, I, p.78.
81 Ashton 1997, no.1.
82 Adolphus 1839, I, pp.275–6.
83 Mathews 1838, I, pp.307 and 428–9,
84 See Mathews 1838, I, p.244.
85 Mathews 1838, I, p.148.
86 Adolphus 1839, I, p.28.
87 Mathews 1838, II, p.52.
88 Mathews 1838, I, pp.294–302.
89 Mathews 1838, I, p.302.
90 Ashton 1997, no.471.
91 Mathews 1838, I, pp.420–1 and II, pp.104–15, see also Ashton 1997, nos.465 and 469.
92 Ashton 1997, no.471.
93 Mathews 1838, I, p.143.
94 J. Lambird, *Home Circuit or Cockney Gleanings*, 1827, quoted in Ashton 1997, introduction.
95 Ashton 1997, nos.465 and 469.
96 Mathews 1838, II, p.112.
97 Mathews 1838, II, p.50.
98 Ashton 1997, no.463
99 Mathews 1838, I, p.127.
100 D. E. Williams, *The Life and Correspondence of Sir Thomas Lawrence*, London 1831, I, p.197.
101 Ashton 1997, no.49.
102 See Dobbs 1972, p.103, and Thomas and Hare 1989, p.368.
103 *The Druriad* quoted in Garrick Catalogue 1909, p.24.
104 See Mathews 1838, I, p.142.
105 W. Archer and R. W. Lowe (eds.), *Dramatic Essays*, London 1894, p.108, quoted in Williamson 1970, p.4.